USING

E-Learning

Here Is How You Can

- Target Specific Business Goals

- Reinvent the Training Function

- Demonstrate Economic Value

ASTD
Linking People,
Learning & Performance

William Horton

Ordering information: Books published by ASTD can be ordered by calling 800.628.2783 or 703.683.8100, or via the Website at www.astd.org.

Library of Congress Catalog Card Number: 2001098293

ISBN: 1-56286-309-6

All figures are printed with permission of William Horton Consulting.

Contents

Preface vii
    What Is This Book About?...vii
    Who Should Read This Book?....................................viii
    How Much Must I Already Know About E-Learning? viii
    How Is This Book Different? viii

Section I: The New World of Training................................1

Chapter 1: The Potential of E-Learning 3
    Using E-Learning for Organizational Purposes 3
    Redefining E-Learning as a Tool 4
    What E-Learning Can Do 5
    What E-Learning Cannot Do......................................11
    Your Turn 12

Section II: Improving Business Effectiveness 15

Chapter 2: Increasing Revenues 17
    Getting to Market Quicker......................................17
    Promoting Products and Services................................20
    Selling Conventional Training 23
    Your Turn 25

Chapter 3: Improving Operations 29
    Improving Workforce Performance 29
    Recruiting and Retaining Better Employees.....................32
    Advancing Specific Employees...................................35
    Smoothing Labor Relations......................................38
    Your Turn...40

Chapter 4: Selling E-Learning 43

What Can You Sell 43

What Is Your Market? 44

Economics of Selling E-Learning 45

Refining Your Business Model 48

How to Sell E-Learning 50

Your Turn 51

Chapter 5: Reducing Costs of Training 55

Can E-Learning Cut Training Costs? 55

Kinds of Costs 55

Delivery Costs 56

Development Costs 59

Infrastructure Costs 63

Travel Costs 66

Opportunity Costs 68

Costs of Informal Coaching 71

Your Turn 73

Section III: Improving the Reach and Quality of Training 79

Chapter 6: Making Training Available to More People 81

Why Make Learning More Widely Available? 81

Busy Workers 83

Distant Workers. 84

Mobile Workers 87

Learners with Language Difficulties 91

Learners of Different Cultures 93

Older Learners 96

Younger Learners 98

Learners with Disabilities 99

Your Turn 107

Chapter 7: Accomplishing General Learning Goals 109

Getting Beginners Started 109

Turning Novices into Experts 115

Activating Self-Directed Learners 119

Increasing Transfer from Training to Work 121

Your Turn 125

Section IV: Reinventing the Training Function..127

Chapter 8: Rethinking the Training Department 129
    Revamping Training's Image..129
    Aligning Training with Organizational Goals 131
    Becoming a Profit Center 135
    Your Turn..139

Chapter 9: Blending E-Learning and Classroom Training...................143
    Why Blend Classroom Training and E-Learning? 143
    Common Forms of Blending...144
    Economics of Blending 148
    Toward a Strategy for Blending 148
    Your Turn..154

Chapter 10: Creating Learning Environments 157
    What Is a Personal Electronic Learning Environment? 157
    Why Build Learning Environments? 158
    Components of a Learning Environment...............................158
    Building an Electronic Learning Environment.......................159
    How Workers Will Learn—a Vision....................................162
    Your Turn..163

References...165
About the Author 169

Preface

Welcome to the post-hype era of e-learning! In the hyper-hyped phase of e-learning's evolution, organizations developed and deployed e-learning because that was the thing to do. Some projects succeeded, but many did not. Claims of 1,000 percent return-on-investment were common but seldom verified by any standard accounting principles. Training, and e-learning in particular, was a world unto itself.

Fast forward to now. Organizations are still intensely interested in e-learning; but to justify the investments in e-learning, they are demanding projects manifestly aligned with high-level and bottom-line corporate objectives. And, they are holding these projects fully accountable for achieving promised results. These demands have been a real wake-up call for organizations and trainers who must now learn to *use* e-learning? This book tells how.

WHAT IS THIS BOOK ABOUT?

Using E-Learning explains how to use e-learning for corporate purposes, not as an end in itself. With this book, you can develop a comprehensive, concrete, and specific strategy for using e-learning in your organization.

This book assumes that the organization has decided to use e-learning and is now interested in how to do so in an effective, efficient, and financially responsible way. This book goes beyond deciding whether to use e-learning. It will guide you in deciding what types of e-learning to use, how much e-learning to implement, how to mix e-learning with other forms of learning and electronic media, and how to implement e-learning projects to accomplish precisely targeted organizational objectives.

Some of the issues discussed here apply at the level of the training department. Others apply at the level of the organization. Some will be ideas you can implement directly. Others will require sharing visions, building alliances, and relentless experimentation.

WHO SHOULD READ THIS BOOK?

This book is for anyone who wants to use e-learning wisely. It is for the person who will be implementing e-learning in an organization, whether he or she is the manager of a training department, a senior staffer charged with leading an e-learning project, a chief learning officer, or even the chief executive officer.

For the corporate training leader, this book tells how to use e-learning to strategically reposition training functions so they clearly and strongly support corporate goals. It details how to execute the traditional goals of training quicker, less expensively, and for more people in the organization. For the corporate executive, it tells how to use e-learning to further organizational goals by increasing profits, smoothing operations, recruiting and retaining talent, and getting to market quicker. If the executives of your organization need to know how e-learning fits into corporate strategies, send them copies of this book.

In short, this book is for anyone who wants training to take a leadership role in the movement to a knowledge society.

HOW MUCH MUST I ALREADY KNOW ABOUT E-LEARNING?

You do not have to be vice president of your information technology department to get the most from this book, but a basic understanding of the technologies and components of e-learning systems would help. If you lack such knowledge, no need to fret. You still need to buy and read this book, but here's how you can get the most out of it: Go to the book's companion Website (www.horton.com/using), and peruse the white paper entitled "Components of E-Learning and Knowledge Management Systems."

This white paper covers the technical elements discussed throughout this book. Generously provided by Katherine Horton of William Horton Consulting, this white paper is an integral part of this book, rounding out the information in section I. If you find yourself wondering "What exactly is an LMS?" or "How do online scavenger hunts work?" download and read this white paper.

HOW IS THIS BOOK DIFFERENT?

With this book, "some assembly is required." E-learning does not work well when used by rote. Effective use of e-learning requires combining its techniques and technologies in ways that fulfill specific goals for each unique situation.

Much of this book consists of checklists of possibilities to consider, ideas to ponder, and practices to avoid. For many crucial issues, you will find a brief explanation of the issue and pointers to resources to help you conduct the research necessary to make a decision appropriate for you and your organization.

In addition, you will find many brief analyses showing the economic consequences of implementing e-learning solutions. You can also go to the book's companion Website to download the spreadsheet containing these analyses so you can crunch your own numbers. (If you find a better way to do these calculations, send your improvements back to the author at william@horton.com.)

Each chapter ends with a section titled "Your Turn," which gives you an opportunity to apply what you have just read. You can write your answers right in the book or download a blank copy of the activity from the book's Website (www.horton.com/using). By completing these activities, you can build a clear plan for using e-learning to accomplish the goals of your organization.

William Horton
January 2002

Section I:
The New World of Training

E-learning is the biggest change to training since the invention of the classroom. It forever alters the economics underlying training and education and offers to overcome difficulties that have bedeviled training for centuries. But, realizing these opportunities will take more than switching from overhead projectors to Web servers. It will take more than money and bandwidth. Realizing the potential of e-learning will require designing and deploying e-learning projects in ways that clearly and substantially advance organizational goals.

E-learning is not a single, one-size-fits-all solution to every problem that besets training today. In fact, treating it as such often causes it to fail to deliver the potential benefits it offers. Realizing those benefits requires understanding what e-learning can accomplish for an organization and its individual employees and customers. And, it requires a clear view of the vast variety of e-learning solutions possible.

Realizing the potential for e-learning will also require honest acknowledgment of the limitations of e-learning and a consequent targeting of tasks for which e-learning is suited. Chapter 1 points out ways that e-learning can fit into your organizational framework to reduce costs and increase revenue while delivering more and better training to learners in less time. With this background, you can begin tailoring e-learning solutions to meet your organization's specific needs.

On this book's companion Website (www.horton.com/using), you will find the second half of section I. Entitled "Components of E-Learning and Knowledge Management Systems," it provides a descriptive menu of e-learning solutions. Not only does it list the array of e-learning technologies available, but it also describes them, gives examples of supporting software, and includes screenshots of some e-learning applications.

1

The Potential of E-Learning

E-learning has been hailed as an educational breakthrough: a true synthesis of humanism and technology, the way learning will take place in the 21st century, and the complete replacement for the obsolete classroom. Reports of 1,000 percent return-on-investment have some executives swooning in their corner offices. Classroom instructors are writing their résumés, and e-learning entrepreneurs are counting their stock options.

Yet, training in the corporate world has changed little; it generally relies upon the centuries-old didactic method. People still congregate in rooms to listen to and watch an instructor dispense wisdom.

Initial experiences with e-learning have shown all rational beings involved that, despite its enormous potential, e-learning is no panacea. Corporate executives and managers are ready for a realistic, common-sense approach to deploying e-learning within their organizations. They demand to know the details and insist on looking behind the curtain. Investments in e-learning must pass the same gauntlet of concerns as other projects clamoring for organizational resources. This book will help you propose e-learning solutions that stand up to the critical scrutiny they are likely to receive.

USING E-LEARNING FOR ORGANIZATIONAL PURPOSES

This book is about using e-learning, not just doing e-learning. E-learning works best as the means to an end, not as an end in itself. The cry of "Let's do some e-learning!" now draws a resounding reply of "Why?" Why indeed? For e-learning to make economical or educational sense, it must be targeted to specific objectives.

Training managers, even zealous e-learning advocates, are recommending more of a surgical approach to e-learning deployments. Rather than promising to replace all conventional training with e-learning within six months, they now suggest targeting the 25 percent best suited for e-learning and ramping up an additional 5 or 10 percent per year. Few talk about conducting all training by e-learning, and many now gush over blended solutions that mix e-learning and conventional methods.

Managers seeking to apply e-learning today must do so with eyes wide open. They must take a realistic view of what e-learning can and cannot do for their organizations, their employees, and their customers. They realize that e-learning projects must be anchored on specific performance objectives that stem directly from sanctioned organizational goals.

The design, development, and delivery of e-learning must proceed with those corporate goals in mind. Projects will be evaluated, not based on smiley-face feedback cards, but on whether the original business goals were accomplished, and the contribution of e-learning to those goals is clear.

E-learning can also be used to accomplish corporate objectives that could be accomplished by other means as well. The movement to e-learning may, however, provide the necessary excuse or serve as a catalyst for changes that you have wanted to make all along.

REDEFINING E-LEARNING AS A TOOL

Some important ideas about e-learning need special emphasis, either because they correct widespread misconceptions or because they further the more sophisticated use of e-learning required to fulfill its promise. These key ideas include the following:

- E-learning is not just courses. E-learning can be packaged in units other than complete courses and can be embedded in, blended with, and infused into other efforts. E-learning lets trainers deliver mini-courses, micro-courses, and nano-courses as they strive to develop truly reusable training components.
- E-learning is not always a noun. E-learning is sometimes a verb, that is, a process. Sometimes it is an adverb, that is, a way of doing things. E-learning is not a particular program or a single technology. It is, however, a way of using tools and technology to stimulate learning.
- E-learning is a collection of processes and technologies, which can be embedded in existing organizational systems and activities, including classroom training, online help, performance support systems, and knowledge management efforts. You can consider e-learning a constituent in such efforts rather than just a stand-alone project.
- E-learning is a solution in search of a problem. E-learning seldom works well when it is the end rather than the means. Organizations must focus on the ends of training before selecting e-learning as the means.

WHAT E-LEARNING CAN DO

Even the accomplishments of early, crude e-learning projects are impressive. E-learning can bring to fruition many different corporate, learning, and personal goals. It is important that you understand the potential benefits of e-learning so that you can choose the ones to initiate and sustain an e-learning project.

For the Organization That Uses E-Learning

E-learning offers an array of benefits to organizations that use e-learning to train their employees and customers. Some of these improve bottom-line profits directly, and others make long-term contributions to the intellectual capital of the organization.

Increase Sales. By making free or low-cost e-learning courses available to customers, an organization can attract and retain customers. The offer of free training will attract potential customers to the organization's Website and entice existing customers to renew contact. Such courses, by better educating customers on the use of products, can inspire trust and demonstrate the value of advanced features available through upgrades and add-on products. Making such substantive training available can win attention in the industry and demonstrate a progressive public spirit.

> ### What Does *Benefit* Mean?
>
> E-learning offers many potential benefits, some of which I describe in this chapter. In subsequent sections of this book, I show how to achieve these benefits. When I say that e-learning can offer some benefit, I mean that the *right type of e-learning, if well designed and executed, can accomplish that benefit.* I do not mean to imply that just doing something in e-learning guarantees that result.
>
> W.H.

Internal training can increase sales, too. By reducing the time required to train an entire salesforce, e-learning will enable the organization to get its products to market sooner and thus have a longer sales cycle. Better-trained sales representatives can more fully answer questions from customers and are more likely to sell newer, more advanced, higher-margin products.

Increase Speed and Flexibility. To thrive in business today, organizations must be nimble. They struggle to bring products to market quicker. They must rapidly adopt new methods, find new markets, and shed old biases. Such shifts require periodic training of masses of people. E-learning can be deployed to the whole organization at once and does not require booking auditoriums, making travel reservations, or training large numbers of trainers.

Improve Workforce Performance. By improving knowledge, skills, attitudes, habits, and methods of workers, e-learning makes the organization more effective and more efficient. But, any form of training could do that. E-learning can be especially effective when it provides just-in-time, just-enough, just-for-me learning that keeps learners on the job more of the time and enables them to quickly identify and fix problems that hold up production or lead to costly errors.

Reduce Time Off the Job for Training. In many complex, rapidly changing businesses, employees must spend considerable time in training. Time off the job is a major drain on the effectiveness of their organizations. E-learning can help by providing custom-tailored training that requires less time to take by eliminating the time required to travel to the site of training and by breaking training into short segments that learners can fit among their regular work duties.

Recruit and Retain Better Employees. Even in tough economic times, recruiting and retaining the best employees is hard. Salary is not the only reason talented people choose one company over another. Other reasons include concerns about potential advancement, work hours, and ability to spend time with family. E-learning can provide the training people need but without travel, which entails overtime for completing backlogs of work and which necessitates spending more time away from their families. These reasons apply especially to overworked, stressed-out, travel-weary corporate trainers.

Initiate and Nurture Knowledge Management Efforts. Training educates individuals. Knowledge management educates the entire organization. By providing universal access to uniform, high-quality training, e-learning becomes a powerful tool for knowledge management. And, because e-learning uses some of the same computer and network technologies already supporting the organization's electronic libraries, best practices databases, and competency assessments, it can readily form the core of an organization's knowledge management efforts.

Advance Targeted Individuals. Many organizations seek to advance targeted individuals within their ranks. These organizations may be trying to fill critical vacancies for managers or technical staff, or they may be trying to redress inequities in the number of women and minorities in higher positions.

Because self-directed e-learning does not require a quorum of learners to form a class and does not require waiting for a class to begin, it is ideal for helping targeted individuals acquire the skills and knowledge they need to advance rapidly. Through e-learning, they do not have to sacrifice the time on the job they need to gain the experience and credibility their new positions require.

Support Those with Disabilities. Many organizations in the United States, Canada, and the European Union are struggling to make their job positions available to those who suffer from common disabilities such as deafness, blindness, or mobility limitations. In the United States, the federal government and organizations that do business with the federal government are required under laws and regulations, such as the Americans with Disabilities Act, the Telecommunications Act, and the 1998 amendments of Section 508 of the Rehabilitation Act, to provide equal access to job positions and information technology resources for those with disabilities.

E-learning, with its ability to use multimedia and to interface with assistive technologies (screen readers, for example), helps make training accessible to many more than could benefit from classroom training. The anonymity of e-learning also lets those with disabilities choose whether to reveal their disability to the instructor or fellow learners.

For the Training Department

Training departments benefit in their own way from a shift to e-learning. E-learning can help them operate more efficiently, train more effectively, and position themselves more appropriately within the larger organization they serve.

Cut the Costs of Training. The ability of e-learning to cut the costs of training is thoroughly documented. Cost reductions of 50 percent or even 90 percent are not hard to find, especially when training a large number of people who would otherwise have to travel to take the training and who already have computers and network connections. E-learning eliminates the need for travel and greatly reduces facility costs.

Train Neglected Learners. Not everyone has access to classroom training. Not everyone learns effectively in the classroom setting. E-learning can provide an alternative for delivering training to the following people:

- remote learners who cannot afford the time or cost of travel to attend conventional training
- busy learners who cannot fit a conventional class into their schedules
- learners who travel and cannot be at the site of training when it occurs
- shy learners who fear embarrassment by an aggressive instructor or classmates
- learners with language difficulties who cannot understand a fast-talking instructor and who are self-conscious about speaking out in class
- learners with disabilities.

For all these learners, e-learning can provide an alternative that fits their abilities, schedule, and budget.

Revitalize Classroom Training. Far from killing off classroom training, e-learning is adding new life to this venerable institution. Web access from the classroom adds a wealth of resources, stimulates interactivity, and supplies current information to make each classroom session different from the last. And, collaborative media like email, chat, and discussion forums extend conversations well beyond normal class hours.

Revamp the Training Department's Image. In many organizations, the perceptions of the training department are years or decades out of date. Too often, trainers are perceived as technophobic reactionaries whose primary method of delivery involves hour-long lectures spoken in a monotone in front of overhead transparencies, each sporting exactly five bullet items. E-learning forces the organization to take a fresh look at training and the department that produces it.

Implement Instructional Strategies. E-learning is highly flexible and theoretically agnostic. The constraints of the classroom format or learners' expectations for the form of training may have limited your use of training strategies or discouraged you from using better models of learning. E-learning provides a new opportunity to do it right. And, e-learning offers new ways to monitor effectiveness so you can quickly adjust your designs and document your successes.

Become a Profit Center. Many training departments are using the shift to e-learning as an opportunity to redefine themselves as profit centers within their organizations. Because e-learning can be delivered less expensively and tracked automatically, training departments find diminishing resistance to shifting training costs from an overhead model to a charge-back model of accounting. Some departments are exploiting e-learning's ease of delivery to make their e-learning courses available to their customers, suppliers, and industry groups for a fee. Needless to say, jumping from the cost column to the revenue column on the organization's balance sheet does wonders for the stature of the training department within the boardroom.

Align Training with Business Purposes. Some training departments are going further. They are using the movement to e-learning as a chance to align their efforts with the basic goals of their organization. By anchoring e-learning projects to clear, sanctioned business goals and by carefully tracking results, these departments demonstrate their direct contribution to the organization's goals.

For Organizations Selling Training

E-learning offers new business opportunities for organizations that sell training. These may be training and consulting firms or internal training departments that are profit centers.

For organizations providing training in esoteric fields where there is little competition, e-learning offers vast new markets. Training providers are not limited to geographic regions. They can provide training to 24 time zones as easily as to one classroom. They can offer training 24 hours a day, seven days a week. Because the delivery costs of e-learning are low, training providers can recoup their investments by training ever larger numbers of learners.

Some organizations, however, are finding that in their market they cannot make money selling e-learning courses directly. Either their potential customers are not ready for e-learning, or the number of potential learners is not high enough to justify developing e-learning courses. Still, such organizations are finding a place for e-learning in their business model. Some use it to promote existing offerings. They may provide a short e-learning course free on their Websites. Such a loss leader draws people to the site and lets them sample the quality of training available from the firm. At the end of the free e-learning course, learners may be invited to enroll, for a fee, in classroom courses.

Other organizations are using e-learning to add a competitive edge to their existing offerings. They may use e-learning to preview the classroom course or to provide a job aid to help learners apply what they learned in the classroom to situations they encounter back on the job.

For Trainers as Individuals

Classroom instructors have reacted in a variety of ways to e-learning. Some have welcomed it as the next evolutionary step, and others have expressed fear, loathing, disgust, disdain, or indifference. Many fear that e-learning will eliminate their jobs as stand-up teachers or eliminate what they enjoy most about that job, but most are coming to realize that e-learning can make their jobs easier, more rewarding, and potentially more lucrative.

Reduced Tedium. Even the best instructors tire of teaching the same course over and over again. They pray for a learner to ask an original question and even welcome the rush they get when the projector bulb burns out. E-learning can take over those tedious duties of teaching routine material. E-learning does not get bored or impatient. It does not wonder to itself: "Why can't these people understand this material? I've explained it 138 times already!" Liberated from teaching routine factual and procedural matter, the e-learning instructor can focus on interacting with learners in creative games, role-playing exercises, and other activities that allow the instructor's technique, style, and experience to shine.

Reduced Travel. As an instructor, your first few out-of-town training assignments may seem like a paid vacation. But, when you are traveling 25 or 50 percent (or more) of the time for several years, the thrill wears off. You beg your boss not to make you leave frozen Minnesota to teach for a week in Hawaii. A request to go to Paris prompts you to threaten resignation.

Many instructors cite the requirements for frequent travel and time away from their families as a major drawback of their job. Several training managers have confided that the burnout rate for trainers who travel is two or three times higher than that of trainers who can hug their families every night.

E-learning can eliminate the need for instructors to travel to the site of training. Trainers can eliminate a great deal of travel time and avoid perpetual jet lag. And, because trainers and facilitators can be anywhere, they can more easily squeeze in vacations and other personal time. When asked why he was interested in e-learning, one corporate trainer replied, "To get a life."

New Careers. Many classroom instructors are in search of new careers. They love teaching but do not want to move into the management of training. E-learning offers another career track where they can apply their communications skills and their knowledge of instructional design. E-learning is a new field rife with opportunities to break new ground. Creativity counts for more than seniority, a melodious voice, or a pretty face.

For Learners

For learners (and those who pay the costs of their training), e-learning offers a more efficient and convenient way to acquire skills and knowledge. Some of the advantages for learners are the following:

- *Less time required for training:* Properly designed e-learning, supplemented with multimedia, can teach more efficiently.
- *More time spent learning:* With e-learning, learners just log in and go. They do not have to drive to the airport, fly across the country, rent a car, check into a hotel, grab a few hours' sleep, drive to the training center, park the car, find the room, and wait for the class to start.
- *Pace tuned to the learner:* E-learners control the pace of their learning. They can go as fast as ambition or curiosity impels them. They can repeat difficult sections they want to master fully.
- *Training tailored to personal needs and interests:* Learners can choose which topics to study in detail and which to skim. They can skim a topic at the beginning of a course and then come back and study it more carefully once its value becomes obvious.

■ *Training more easily fit into a busy, irregular schedule:* E-learning can be taken anywhere there's a computer connected to the Internet. Learners can learn while in their offices, in a corporate training center, from home, or from a laptop in a hotel room while traveling.

E-learning especially benefits motivated learners striving to meet their own business or personal goals.

For Users of the Organization's Products

E-learning enhances the experience of using many products on the market, especially knowledge products such as computer software, communications devices, and electronic equipment. These benefits splash back onto the suppliers of such products in the form of increased sales and reduced support costs.

The availability of simple tutorials, guided tours, and other usage aids ensures that customers can make immediate use of a product and painlessly progress to using advanced features. By integrating training, documentation, and support to produce electronic performance support systems, the trainer can add practical value to products.

WHAT E-LEARNING CANNOT DO

One of the first steps of any successful project is setting realistic expectations. Although e-learning can work miracles, it cannot work all miracles at once. Nor is it without costs, not the least of which is the requirement to think about training in new ways.

Deliver All Advantages at Once

E-learning can do all of the wonderful things already mentioned, but it cannot do them all simultaneously on a single project. Understand that there are tradeoffs among the benefits of e-learning. For example, if you want the deeper learning possible with rich collaboration among fellow learners, you may have to sacrifice the ability of learners to set their own pace and agenda. The use of rich media requires fast network connections, which may rule out learners whose travel computer has only a slow modem.

Deliver Advantages without Cost

E-learning can save vaults of money—sometimes—but usually only after a sizeable up-front investment. The low delivery costs of e-learning are usually purchased with high development costs. Many of the costs of e-learning are hidden. These may include the money learners must spend to upgrade their computers and the time they spend downloading and installing necessary software and plug-ins.

Two hidden costs are risk and anxiety. Like all endeavors that depend on imaginative applications of rapidly advancing technology, e-learning projects have an element of risk. Even the best-managed projects sometimes fail. E-learning pioneers must have the self-confidence and organizational support to withstand such failures.

The other hidden cost is the anxiety of teaching in new ways. Classroom training draws upon hundreds of years of evolution and refinement. Learners and trainers fully understand how classroom training works. For e-learning, no such uniform model exists—or is even possible given the rate of advancement of e-learning. All this change and uncertainty is stressful to all participants.

Deliver Advantages without Fundamental Change

Trainers can implement e-learning to carry on the old ways of training, but merely mimicking what has worked in the past will not exploit the full potential of e-learning. To achieve the full advantages of e-learning, be prepared to change the following:

- *How you package and deliver training:* More and more training will be created in modules, which buyers of training or even individual learners can mix and match for specific learning goals.
- *The people you employ:* E-learning, at least at its current state of development, requires strong technical skills and a fundamental knowledge of instructional design. It craves innovative designers who go beyond imitation of established forms of training.
- *The way you think about training:* For hundreds of years, education and training have been activities pursued at the beginning of life or at the beginning of a new job. Training now must be considered a continual, daily, or even hourly activity.
- *Delivering knowledge solutions, not just training courses:* Solutions may require integrating collaboration systems, information repositories, best practices databases, and other components not traditionally thought of as training. Training is no longer a self-contained activity.

◀◀ ◀◀ ◀◀ ◀◀ ◀◀ ▶▶ ▶▶ ▶▶ ▶▶ ▶▶

YOUR TURN

At the end of each chapter, you will find an opportunity to adapt what you just read about to your situation. By completing these activities, you can assemble a personal plan for using e-learning.

You can write your answers right in the book. If you are squeamish about defacing such a fine book, photocopy the "Your Turn" sections. The copyright police will not e-arrest you. Or, you can download a copy of all the "Your Turn" sections from this book's companion Website (www.horton.com/using) and print them out.

How Can E-Learning Help Your Organization Deliver Training?

Worksheet 1-1 lists the ways that e-learning can benefit organizations that use it. Which of these benefits is important to your organization? Identify the ones that are important to your organization and assign them a numerical priority, 10 being highest, and 1 being lowest.

Worksheet 1-1. Benefits for organizations using e-learning.

Benefit	Important to Your Organization? (Yes/No)	Priority (10 = Highest, 1 = Lowest)
Benefits to the Organization as a Whole		
Increase sales		
Increase organizational speed and flexibility		
Improve work performance		
Reduce time off the job for training		
Recruit and retain better employees		
Initiate and nurture knowledge management activities		
Support fast-track and affirmative action programs		
Open job positions to those with disabilities		
Benefits to the Training Department		
Cut the costs of training		
Train those not well served by conventional training		
Revitalize classroom training		
Revamp the training department's image		
Implement particular instructional strategies		
Become more of a profit center		
Align training with business purposes		

How Can E-Learning Benefit Individuals?

E-learning can benefit those who take training, those who conduct training, and those who use products supported by e-learning. Worksheet 1-2 lists these individuals. For each group, specify what you believe will be the main benefit of e-learning.

Worksheet 1-2. Benefits for individuals using e-learning.

Group	Main Benefit
Instructors, trainers, and teachers	
Learners	
Users of products supported by e-learning	

What Fundamental Changes Will E-Learning Require?

To reap the benefits of e-learning, people in your organization will have to make fundamental changes in the ways they create, deliver, and possibly think about training. In worksheet 1-3, list a few of these changes and who must make them.

Worksheet 1-3. Fundamental changes required to implement e-learning.

Change in the Way Training Is Created, Delivered, and Thought About	Who Must Make This Change?

Section II:
Improving Business Effectiveness

Direct contributions to profit are highly valued by upper management, but demonstrating the directness of training's contributions is hard.

Making money is simple. The formula for business profit does not contain any exponents or Greek letters or even long division; it is minimalism itself:

$$\text{Profit} = \text{Revenues} - \text{Costs}$$

Revenues are the money taken in, and costs are the money paid out. What is left over is profit. Of course, achieving an excess of revenues over costs is not so simple.

This section shows how to spot opportunities to contribute to the bottom-line profits of organizations, how to demonstrate and quantify those contributions, and how to design and deploy e-learning to ensure these contributions. It reveals four main ways that e-learning can improve business effectiveness:

- by increasing revenues
- by improving operations
- by selling e-learning
- by reducing the costs of training within the organization.

The first two chapters of this section demonstrate e-learning's contribution at the corporate level. Chapter 2 shows how to use e-learning to directly increase revenues, and chapter 3 shows how to use e-learning to improve operations and thereby reduce costs.

The next two chapters explain uses of e-learning at the level of the training department. Chapter 4 suggests how to raise revenues by making a business of e-learning. Chapter 5 tackles the cost side of the equation by showing how to use e-learning to reduce the costs of training.

2

Increasing Revenues

E-learning can tune up, tweak, and turbocharge revenue-generating activities of a company. This chapter considers how e-learning can increase revenues produced by an organization's current activities. It shows how e-learning can help get products to market sooner, promote sales of products, and increase sales of conventional training offerings.

GETTING TO MARKET QUICKER

Getting products to market quickly is critical for rapidly advancing and highly competitive businesses. Companies that do so can sell products over a longer period of time. And, they can sell those products while they have unique advantages that demand a premium profit margin. Getting products to market first establishes leadership and draws attention to the company and its entire product line.

Some management consultants suggest that speed in developing products is the most important factor in business success today. It is easy to see why when you contemplate companies like Sun Microsystems and 3Com, which derive 80 percent or more of their revenue from products less than a year old (Peters, 2001).

Economics of Getting to Market Quicker

Take a look at how being first to market benefits a company economically. A hypothetical company, e-Femoral, develops and sells medical electronics, a highly competitive and rapidly advancing field.

In this field, products go through three phases of sales. If they are unique and have no direct competition, they garner high profits. e-Femoral estimates that during this phase, its products could return $500,000 per month in profits. When competitive products are introduced, the product is still a current-generation product, but it must sell against competition. Profits during this phase are expected to be $300,000 per month. After about a year, next-generation products will be introduced, and the product must be sold as past-generation. During this phase, profits are expected to be about $100,000 per month.

Currently e-Femoral expects to launch its product two months after its main competitor. Ten months later, next-generation products will be launched. Thus, e-Femoral will be able to sell its product for 10 months as a current-generation product. During this time, it will collect $300,000 per month in profits. After next-generation products are introduced, e-Femoral expects to be able to continue selling its product for 12 more months, collecting $100,000 per month in profit. Total profits are thus expected to be $4.2 million.

But the CEO of e-Femoral, Charles "Bones" Magee, wants to accelerate the product introduction by four months, beating the competition to the market by two months. For two months, e-Femoral's product will be unique and earn $500,000 per month in profits. In addition, it will be current-generation for 12 months rather than just 10 months, adding another two months of $300,000 per month to the till. Launching the product four months earlier thus increases profits by $1.6 million or 38 percent.

Table 2-1 summarizes this analysis. As always, you can download this spreadsheet from the companion Website (www.horton.com/using) and perform your own calculations. What would happen if e-Femoral could beat the competition to market by three months instead of two months? What if the monthly profit during the unique phase were $400,000?

Table 2-1. Value of getting to market quicker.

Phase	Monthly Profit	Scenario A		Scenario B	
		Months	Profit	Months	Profit
Unique (no competition)	$500,000	0	$0	2	$1,000,000
First generation (with competition)	$300,000	10	$3,000,000	12	$3,600,000
Second generation	$100,000	12	$1,200,000	12	$1,200,000
Total			**$4,200,000**		**$5,800,000**

How E-Learning Saves Time

E-learning can help if training is in any way a bottleneck along the critical path of developing and launching new products and services. E-learning allows companies to develop and deploy training quicker. Cisco cut the time to get new manufacturing workers up to full productivity from 12 weeks to four weeks (Hall, 2000a). Some organizations require training delivery to begin a mere 48 hours after the CEO announces a new product.

For widely dispersed organizations, e-learning can update and inform employees and customers globally. Hewlett-Packard reduced the time required to train a global salesforce from one year to 30 days (Picard, 1996). In so doing, the corporation cut training costs by 78 percent.

Now look at an example of how e-learning might get a product to market sooner. One common bottleneck in introducing products to the market is the time required to train a global salesforce. e-Femoral plans to introduce its new line of medical devices, but first it must train its salesforce. They plan to do so by sending the sales training team, including the product manager, vice president of sales, and head of development, on a world tour of sales offices.

For each office, the team will have to travel to the office and set up the rooms for training (one day), conduct formal training (two days), conduct follow-up meetings to clear up remaining issues and answer questions (one day), and fly home (one day). Each office will thus take five days, or one workweek. Because e-Femoral has 15 offices, training in all offices will require 15 workweeks.

Greta Groundswell, head of training, proposes conducting training by e-learning. Her plan includes having sales representatives spend a day reviewing marketing materials. After this step, they will have two days of Web-conducted briefings using online meeting software that allows presenters to share documents, draw pictures, and take questions from the audience. To ensure that they are ready to begin selling, sales representatives then spend a day taking online assessments and working in sales simulations. Over the next 12 business days, sales representatives and headquarters staff will discuss the new product line using online discussions. The total time for e-learning is thus 16 days or 3.2 workweeks. E-learning saves 11.8 workweeks in getting e-Femoral's product to market.

Table 2-2 summarizes this analysis. Think you can do better? Then download the spreadsheet from the book's companion Website (www.horton .com/using) and give it a try. What if the product were especially complex and required more time for the training? What if the follow-up online discussion takes twice as long?

Using E-Learning to Get to Market Quicker

In getting products to market, there is little time to prepare and deliver training. To reduce time to market, use e-learning to streamline production and make compromises where necessary:

☐ Prioritize training. Provide training on just what is needed to launch and begin selling the product. Teach the key facts, figures, and concepts—and how to find answers in extensive online information you also provide.

☐ Use existing materials. Revamp materials from product development, marketing, documentation, support, sales, advertising, and other departments. Hire a fast editor and a quick-draw artist. Add some assessment and feedback tools.

☐ Buy or rent courses and components to cover generic subjects. Customize them to your needs but do not waste time developing what someone else has already perfected.

☐ Use conferencing technology for sales briefings. An animated speaker is as effective as laboriously produced multimedia, and rich human-human interaction is as effective as human-computer interaction.

☐ Use discussion forums, chat sessions, and instant messaging so learners can ask questions. That way your training does not have to be 100 percent complete.

☐ Streamline production. Prepare templates, style sheets, boilerplate text, and graphics ahead of time. Develop automated techniques to convert common file formats such as Microsoft Word and PowerPoint.

☐ Record experts to provide instant presentations. Subject matter experts may be in short supply because they are critical to the project. Use their time wisely. Set up a portable video and audio recording studio to record experts in their offices.

PROMOTING PRODUCTS AND SERVICES

E-learning can be used to promote your organization's regular products and services. It can help draw attention to products and services, add value to them, make them more enticing to customers, and help them command higher prices.

How E-Learning Can Help

E-learning can make it easier for customers to learn about products, and it can make it less expensive for producers to promote those products. With e-learning, potential customers can, at any time, learn in detail about a product without having to confront a pushy sales representative. The offer of free e-learning can draw

Table 2-2. How e-learning reduces time to market.

With Conventional Training

Travel to the office	1 day
Conduct training	2 days
Follow-up meetings	1 day
Return home	1 day
= Time per office	5 days
× Sales offices	15 offices
= Total time required	75 days
	15 workweeks

With E-Learning

Prestudy of marketing materials	1 day
Presentations and Q&A	2 days
Testing and sales simulations	1 day
Follow-up online discussions	12 days
= Total time required	16 days
	3.2 workweeks
Time Saved	**11.8 workweeks**

people to a company's Website. Macromedia (www.macromedia.com) and Microsoft (www.microsoft.com) frequently offer free courses on their products and technologies at their Websites. E-learning can also expand markets for products by helping customers appreciate the value in the company's products, especially advanced features and add-ons for basic products.

E-learning can also make it easier to learn to use products, thereby enhancing their reputation as easy to use. Nokia, for example, makes training on features of its mobile telephones available over the Web (www.nokiahowto.com). Customers know that ease of use lowers a product's total cost of ownership.

Economics of Promoting Products and Services

Examine how offering free e-learning can increase overall profits. Take the case of Cornered Market Software. True to its name, Cornered Market is the dominant provider of software in its market. The only way it can make money is by selling upgrades for its current product. How might e-learning help?

Cornered Market estimates that 300,000 potential customers have the network connections to take e-learning and that 5 percent of them will respond to an email invitation to do so. That means 15,000 potential customers will take e-learning.

The marketing department projects that after taking e-learning, 40 percent of customers will purchase upgrades, whereas only 25 percent of customers who do not take the e-learning will upgrade. The implication is that of the 15,000 potential customers who take e-learning, 15 percent more of those will upgrade as a result. Cornered Market will, as a result, sell an additional 2,250 upgrades.

As each upgrade fetches a profit of $100, additional profits are $225,000. "Not so fast," you say. "We still have to subtract the costs of the e-learning program." So, make those $150,000, including the costs of developing the e-learning, hosting it, and sending out email invitations to online customers. The net profit from the e-learning venture is thus $75,000.

Table 2-3 summarizes this analysis. You are welcome to download the spreadsheet from the book's Website (www.horton.com/using) and explore the economics of using e-learning to promote products and services. What if 10 percent opt to take the e-learning, but only 30 percent of those who do so purchase the upgrade? What if only 20 percent would have upgraded?

Table 2-3. How free e-learning promotes products.

Potential customers online	300,000	customers
× Fraction who will take e-learning	5%	
= Number who will take e-learning	15,000	customers
Will purchase after taking e-learning	40%	
− Would have purchased anyway	25%	
= Additional sales percentage	15%	
Additional sales	2,250	units
× Profit per unit sold	$100	per unit sold
= Additional profit from sales	$225,000	
− Cost of e-learning program	150,000	
= Net additional profit	$75,000	

Using E-Learning to Promote Products and Services

To use e-learning to promote products and services, use it first to help the sales-force sell better and second to help customers sell themselves on your products. Here are some e-learning offerings you can use to enhance product sales:

- ☐ overview courses to point out the advantages of the product
- ☐ courses on "What's new in this version" to motivate upgrades
- ☐ guided tours to introduce the product and get customers started successfully

- [ ] sales briefings to prepare sales representatives to begin selling the product
- [ ] "Using Product *X* to solve Problem *Y*" mini-courses to show how the product can be used to solve problems important to customers
- [ ] training on advanced features to increase the perceived value of the product.

Advertise availability of your free or low-cost e-learning. Place announcements on your homepage. Send out email announcements to potential customers. Feature e-learning in print and television advertising. Remember to link your e-learning to e-commerce so motivated customers can order at the click of a button. And, link e-commerce to e-learning so potential customers can learn why they should order.

SELLING CONVENTIONAL TRAINING

Chapter 4 suggests how you can make money selling e-learning, but e-learning can also enhance sales of your conventional training at higher profit margins. You can use e-learning technologies and techniques to add value to classroom courses, making them more concise, more capable, and more fun. You may also want to use e-learning as a loss leader for classroom courses, drawing attention to your classroom courses and demonstrating your ability to deliver effective training. If your ability to deliver classroom training is constrained by availability of instructors or classrooms, perhaps you should use e-learning to teach more routine, lower-profit courses, thus freeing resources for more valuable courses.

Economics of Selling Conventional Training

Look at an example of how offering e-learning for free can increase profits for classroom training. Classes-R-Us has very popular classroom courses. They offer classes 100 times per year. Each offering yields $5,000 profit. From these offerings, they derive $500,000 profit per year.

They believe that offering e-learning will draw attention to their classroom training, demonstrate their superb instructional quality, and free up instructors who were teaching break-even courses anyway. They estimate that e-learning will enable them to sell 15 percent more course offerings per year. The 15 new offerings each contribute an additional $5,000 to profits for a boost of $75,000 to the total classroom profits. From this figure is subtracted the annualized cost of developing and offering e-learning. Assume that the cost is $50,000. That means investing in e-learning yields an additional $25,000 per year in profits.

Table 2-4 summarizes this analysis. Different assumptions lead to different results. Why not try out some variations in this calculation by downloading the spreadsheet from the companion Website (www.horton.com/using)? What if the e-learning cost $150,000 to develop? What if the current rate of classroom offerings were 200 classes per year?

Table 2-4. Using e-learning to sell additional classroom courses.

Classroom offerings	100	per year
× Profit per offering	$5,000	per offering
= Current annual profit	$500,000	per year
Additional classroom sales	15%	
Additional classroom courses	15	
Additional classroom profit	$75,000	per year
− Annualized cost of e-learning	$50,000	per year
= Total additional profit	$25,000	

Using E-Learning to Sell Conventional Training

E-learning offers several strategies for enhancing profits from conventional classroom training operations. You can use it to enhance conventional offerings, to attract more customers to training, and to free up critical resources. Discussed below are ways you can deploy e-learning in each of these strategies.

Enhancing Conventional Offerings. E-learning can make conventional training offerings more attractive and more efficient, meaning you can charge more for them, and they cost less to offer. Here are some ideas for using e-learning techniques and technologies to increase the profit margins of your conventional training offerings:

- ☐ Use e-learning to conduct preclass briefings. When learners subsequently show up in the classroom, they have prerequisite knowledge, understand the purpose of the course, and are ready to begin. The resulting classroom sessions are more focused, better organized, and more effective.
- ☐ Use multimedia demonstrations and exercises in the classroom. Simulations, learning games and activities, and dynamic presentations designed for e-learning can easily be adapted for use by instructors in the classroom.
- ☐ Use e-learning collaboration mechanisms for follow-up and transfer. Let learners stay in touch with their instructor and fellow learners after the classroom sessions. Let them ask questions and seek advice as they begin applying what they learned to their jobs.

Attracting Customers. Many organizations are using e-learning courses as loss leaders for their classroom training. The term *loss leader* refers to a product that is sold at a loss just to get customers into the store where they will buy other highly profitable items. To this end, you can use e-learning to demonstrate your company's competence in instructional design, subject matter knowledge, and technical wizardry. In designing loss leader courses:

☐ Focus on something your market wants to learn. Although the course is free, customers must dedicate the time to take it. Make sure that customers learn something of value to them.

☐ Demonstrate superb instructional design skills. Remember that the e-learning course is an introduction to your company. What does it imply about your instructional approach, attention to detail, and understanding of the subject matter?

☐ Keep the course small with clear, constrained objectives. Your goal is not to satiate customers but to give them a taste that piques their appetite for more. Trying to teach too much can inflate development costs, too.

☐ Funnel into your conventional offerings. At appropriate places in e-learning, mention classroom training offerings. Hyperlink to course descriptions and registration forms.

Freeing Up Critical Resources. Some classroom courses are more profitable than others. Some organizations cannot deliver popular courses as quickly as needed. E-learning can help by freeing up classrooms, instructors, and calendar dates. To this end, identify the constraints and use e-learning to overcome those constraints by doing the following:

☐ Compensate for a lack of qualified instructors by converting routine courses to learner-led e-learning or lightly facilitated e-learning.

☐ Reduce the demand for precious classroom space by using conferencing technologies to Webcast conventional courses. That way, instructors can teach from their offices, and learners can take the course from their desks.

☐ Avoid the cost and inconvenience of learners and instructors having to travel to the training site. Use asynchronous e-learning so that learners and instructors in 24 time zones can participate.

◀◀ ◀◀ ◀◀ ◀◀ ◀◀ ▶▶ ▶▶ ▶▶ ▶▶ ▶▶

YOUR TURN

In this segment, you plan how you will use e-learning to increase revenues.

Get to Market Sooner

What product do you need to get to market sooner? How can you use e-learning to get your organization's products to market quicker? Sketch out your plan on worksheet 2-1, and then go on to identify potential uses of e-learning to speed up your project. Using techniques, such as those in this chapter, estimate the economic benefit of completing the project sooner. Model your calculations after the spreadsheets on the companion Website (www.horton .com/using) if you wish.

Worksheet 2-1. Using e-learning to complete a project more quickly.

Pick a project you need to complete more quickly. List it here:

How will e-learning help? List some ways you can use e-learning for your project and estimate how much time each will save.

Use of E-Learning	Time Saved
Total Time Saved	

Using techniques such as those in this chapter, estimate the economic benefit of completing the project earlier.	
Economic Benefit of Earlier Project Completion	$

Promote Products and Services

Consider how you can use e-learning to increase sales of nontraining products and services. In worksheet 2-2, list these items, state how you will use e-learning to promote their sales, and estimate the additional revenue this will generate.

Worksheet 2-2. How e-learning will promote sales of products and services.				

Product or Service	How to Use E-Learning to Promote Its Sales	Current Sales	% Increase	$ Increase
		$	%	$
		$	%	$
		$	%	$
		$	%	$
		$	%	$
			Total Increase	$

Promote Sales of Conventional Training

How can you use e-learning to increase your sales of conventional training? Sketch out your plan in worksheet 2-3.

Worksheet 2-3. Plan for promoting sales of conventional training.

For which conventional training offerings do you want to increase sales? List them here:
By how much: _____%
How much will this percentage increase revenue in dollars? $ _____ per year
How will you use e-learning to accomplish this objective?

3

Improving Operations

E-learning can make organizations more productive and efficient. It can improve the performance of individuals, teams, and the workforce as a whole. E-learning can serve as a tool for recruiting and retaining better employees. It can help accelerate the advancement of exceptional employees. And, it can smooth labor relations. This chapter suggests ways you can use e-learning to accomplish goals like these.

IMPROVING WORKFORCE PERFORMANCE

Your organization probably has programs under way to improve the performance of its workforce. These programs may include efforts to increase the productivity of individuals, improve decision-making skills, streamline processes, reduce errors and accidents, instill organizational values, capture intellectual property, and increase flexibility to seize opportunities. E-learning should be a tool in these efforts.

How E-Learning Can Help

Like any form of training, e-learning can improve employees' abilities to do their jobs, thus reducing inefficiency, accidents, errors, frustration, and confusion. Properly designed and deployed, e-learning can deliver training more quickly and consistently than conventional classroom training or informal "water cooler" training.

E-learning increases the flexibility of organizations to meet new challenges. It can be used to train many people at once or to train individuals as they undertake new jobs. E-learning can be targeted for workers with rare needs, for example where it is not economical to train a whole department with different duties. E-learning does not require travel; therefore, learners spend less time off the job.

Economics of Workforce Performance

Continual improvements in productivity are a mainstay of business and economic success. Over the past 110 years, the productivity of manual work has increased 50 times (Drucker, 1994). It is important to realize the leveraging effects of even small increases in productivity and how e-learning can generate those increases.

Effect of Productivity on Profit. Look at an example of how a small boost in productivity can send profits soaring. A company, call it Greenspan Industries, can sell its products or services for $100 per unit. Producing each unit costs $70, and other costs (sales, administration, advertising) account for an additional $20 of the selling price. This means the company makes $10 per unit in profit.

What would be the effect of a modest improvement in productivity, say 5 percent? Well, a 5 percent improvement would lower the production costs by $3.50, increasing profits by the same amount to $13.50. Thus, a 5 percent increase in productivity yields a 35 percent increase in bottom-line profits. That's why executives and the Federal Reserve chairman seem fixated on productivity.

Table 3-1 summarizes this analysis. If you think the numbers given here are fanciful, go to this book's Website (www.horton.com/using), find the spreadsheet, and plug in numbers that reflect your situation. Or try some variations in this model, like changing the productivity increase and the base production costs.

Table 3-1. Effects of productivity on profit.

Selling price	$100.00	per unit
— Production costs	$70.00	per unit
— Other costs	$20.00	per unit
= Profit	$10.00	per unit
Efficiency increase	5%	
New production costs	$66.50	per unit
New profit	$13.50	per unit
Increase in profits	35%	

E-Learning's Contribution to Profit. How can e-learning contribute to productivity? By better training workers, it can reduce errors, omissions, inefficiency, rework, and indecision. Alternatively, it can simply reduce the time off the job required for training.

Here's an example of how reducing time off the job improves productivity. Assume that at Greenspan Industries employees normally work 2,000 hours per year; less if they have plentiful vacation time, more if they put in overtime.

But not all of that time at work is really time on the job. Employees may be off the job for formal training classes, say 40 hours per year. They may also spend time in informal training, for example being coached and tutored by their supervisors and co-workers. They may also spend time tutoring and coaching others. Now, assume that this informal training amounts to 120 hours per year. In addition, employees may be off work because of preventable accidents, say four hours. More time may be lost due to "mental health" days, that is, time taken off the job due to frustration, anger, and discouragement. This time off shows up as increased sick days, tardiness, and personal business conducted on company time. Assume that mental health days cost 20 hours per year. Add these figures up and you will see that the average Greenspan Industries employee spends 184 hours per year off the job and, hence, works only 1,816 hours per year.

Suppose that e-learning can reduce time off the job by conducting training more efficiently and by delivering more of that training near the site of work. Also assume that it can reduce accidents and injuries by better conducting safety training and can reduce mental health days by better preparing learners for their jobs and work conditions. All in all, suppose that e-learning can reduce time off the job by 40 percent, in effect, adding 73.6 work hours per year. These additional work hours alone boost efficiency by 4 percent.

Table 3-2 summarizes this analysis. Feel free to experiment with different assumptions. You can do so using the spreadsheet, which you can download from the companion Website (www.horton.com/using). Try more modest and more aggressive assumptions about e-learning's contributions. Plug your results into the previous spreadsheet to see the effect on profit.

Table 3-2. E-learning's contribution to productivity.

Normal work hours	2,000	hours per year
Formal training	40	hours per year
Informal training	120	hours per year
Accidents and injuries	4	hours per year
"Mental health" days	20	hours per year
Subtotal	184	hours per year
Actual work hours	1,816	hours per year
Reduction in time off job	40%	
Reclaimed work hours	73.6	hours per year
Increase in productivity	4%	

Using E-Learning to Improve Workforce Performance

To use e-learning to improve workforce performance, consider these approaches:

☐ Target barriers to performance. These may be knowledge, attitudes, beliefs, or skills. Use online tests and surveys to identify the developmental needs of workers.

☐ Buy or rent access to short courses for people with unique training needs.

☐ Use multimedia to improve the effectiveness and persuasiveness of conceptual training.

☐ Customize training to the needs of the department, work team, or individual.

☐ Create custom menus for training materials. Incorporate indexes and search mechanisms to let learners find what they want to learn when they need it.

☐ Deploy self-directed or lightly facilitated e-learning to enable large numbers of workers to acquire skills needed for the organization to change direction rapidly.

☐ Use simulations to let workers practice dangerous or critical activities without risk to life, limb, work flow, or ego.

☐ Provide job aids and embedded training to aid in decision making.

☐ Get the most out of your intellectual property. Repackage and link to components of e-learning content for use in quick-reference summaries, help files, files of frequently asked questions, presentations, and classroom training.

RECRUITING AND RETAINING BETTER EMPLOYEES

Retaining skilled employees and quickly training new hires is a top organizational priority everywhere.

Employee turnover is a critical problem in many industries. According to knowledge management expert Tom Stewart, speaking at ASTD's 2000 International Conference & Exposition, each percentage point reduction in employee turnover saves a *Fortune* 500 company more than $25 million. Costs of recruiting and initially training employees are likewise high. The U.S. Army spends $11,000 per recruit and still fails to meet its recruiting goals (National Center for Policy Analysis, 2001).

In clerical professions, high turnover rates were tolerated in the past because these positions required relatively short training periods, but such is not the case today. Bank tellers and hotel clerks now must learn to operate complex computer systems and must comply with complex legal rules and regulations.

In fact, most jobs today require advanced business and technical skills. The need for advanced education is soaring. In 1950, only 20 percent of jobs required skills beyond those taught in high school. By 1991, the requirement for advanced skills had risen to 65 percent. By 2000, it stood at more than 85 percent (Web-Based Education Commission, 2000). And those skills have a short shelf life. Half of workers' skills are outdated within three to five years (Moe & Blodgett, 2000).

If current trends continue, by 2006 almost half of American workers will either produce information technology products and services or depend on them to perform their work (Henry et al., 1999).

How E-Learning Can Help

Good training, of any form, can help recruit and retain talented employees. Clearly employees value training. A survey conducted by the Gallup Organization of 1,012 U.S. workers in May and June of 1998 found that 99 percent of them believed they needed additional training (Schaaf, 1998). Several studies have found that young workers may not feel loyalty to a company but dearly desire to gain skills (Ruch, 2000).

E-learning is well suited to provide just the kind of training that employees value. The Gallup Organization survey of American workers found that they strongly preferred informal on-the-job training and self-paced training to formal classroom training (Schaaf, 1998).

Training makes the job easier and more satisfying. It can qualify the learner for promotion. Advancement in a training program may provide satisfaction in lieu of job promotion. It can become a visible sign of progress. E-learning can provide immediate access to a wide variety of short training experiences, thus relieving job tedium and the frustration of having to wait to take training. Collaborative learning can introduce new hires to their fellow employees and make them feel part of a community. It can help them make friends and locate peers.

> ### Case in Point: U.S. Army
>
> The U.S. Army is using e-learning to attract and retain the best soldiers. The Army University Access Online (http://eARMYU.com), a $600 million program, promises to let recruits "learn while you serve." It provides anytime-anyplace training that soldiers can take from provided laptop computers. The option is proving popular with Army personnel, who are frequently transferred from post to post and whose job duties rule out conventional training schedules (Web-Based Education Commission, 2000).

Economics of Recruiting and Retaining Employees

To see the potential for e-learning to reduce the costs of employee turnover, look at a simple example. For certain job categories, the Tal&Ted Agency has determined that it costs $5,000 to recruit an employee. This cost reflects the direct costs of advertising for the job and the time of employees who review résumés and applications, interview candidates, and process the employment offer. In addition, initial training costs $5,000. This cost covers the employee's time while in training, the cost of the training itself, and time of supervisors and fellow employees in orienting and coaching the new employee. Therefore, each time an employee must be replaced, the costs add up to $10,000. Also assume that turnover in this job category occurs every 18 months. That means that Tal&Ted pays this $10,000 cost every 18 months. Reduced to an annual basis, you can see that the Tal&Ted Agency pays $6,667 per employee per year for turnover costs.

Nora Risingstar, vice president of human resources, wants to use e-learning to reduce those costs. By featuring rich learning opportunities, the company might attract better candidates and reduce recruiting costs by 10 percent, thus lower recruiting costs to $4,500. E-learning could also deliver that initial training more efficiently, say at a cost of $3,000 instead of $5,000. These savings reduce the turnover cost from $10,000 to $7,500. Furthermore, you may assume that e-learning, by providing opportunities for advancement and reducing confusion and frustration, increases job tenure from 18 months to 24 months. This way, the company must pay the turnover cost only every two years, reducing the annual turnover cost to $3,750 per employee, netting savings of $2,917 per employee per year.

Table 3-3 summarizes this analysis. Feel free to experiment with these figures to see what they would be in your case. You can download a spreadsheet containing this calculation from the companion Website (www.horton .com/using). What would happen if recruiting and initial training costs were reduced further? What if turnover time was not changed?

Table 3-3. Using e-learning to reduce turnover costs.

	Before	After	Savings
Recruiting costs	$5,000	$4,500	$500 per employee
Initial training costs	$5,000	$3,000	$2,000 per employee
Total turnover costs	$10,000	$7,500	$2,500 per employee
Turnover time	18	24	months
Annual turnover costs	$6,667	$3,750	$2,917 per employee

Using E-Learning to Recruit and Retain Employees

To use e-learning to recruit and retain employees, think of how you can make working in your organization more attractive, satisfying, and open ended. Link outcomes of e-learning to employees' goals such as promotions, new careers, enjoyable work, and job security. Some suggestions follow:

- ☐ Publicize the opportunities for growth and development within your organization. Show employees you have not only the careers they want but also the training to advance in those careers. Show screen snapshots in recruiting.

- ☐ Establish virtual corporate universities to make e-learning systematic and visible.

- ☐ Subscribe to training portals to provide access to a wide variety of short courses that learners can take to acquire skills needed immediately, to advance in their career paths, or just to pursue personal interests.

- ☐ Make clear to everyone in the organization that taking e-learning is a sanctioned organizational activity, that it's not like watching television on the job.

- ☐ Tie e-learning directly to job positions. In online job descriptions, link to e-learning courses providing the skills needed for the job. Feature e-learning offerings to qualify workers for difficult-to-fill job positions.

- ☐ If high turnover is inevitable, focus training on specific job duties that will be performed during the person's tenure.

- ☐ Make sure e-learning works on computers that employees have access to. In banks, hospitals, and hotels, these may not be the most advanced systems. The same is true for home systems.

- ☐ Make training fun. Incorporate instructionally sound learning games and simulations (Prensky, 1998). Include rich interactivity and human-human interaction in e-learning.

- ☐ Expand your e-learning curriculum to include life skills, such as parenting, investing, and buying a house. Contract with portals to provide access to courses of interest to spouses and children, too.

- ☐ Award diplomas, certificates, and other tokens that make learning tangible within the company.

> ### Free Advice and Worth the Price
>
> Are you just training the future employees of your competitors? Several of our clients have expressed a concern that providing training on other than the employee's immediate job duties will only prepare them to jump to a competitor. If this is your fear, or if high turnover is inevitable, focus your training on specific job duties that will be performed during the employee's tenure with your company.
>
> Or just ask yourself whether you would rather train employees for future jobs and lose a few of them or not train your employees and lose a lot of them.
>
> W.H.

ADVANCING SPECIFIC EMPLOYEES

Many organizations need to speed up the advancement of certain groups of employees. Such fast-track programs aim at preparing a targeted group of employees to move into advanced job positions. Some such efforts are part of affirmative action projects that aim at redressing underrepresentation of minorities and women at higher levels of management or in specific technical professions. Other efforts are aimed at initiating family members into a family business or transferring leadership to a new generation. Still other efforts just try to fill critical job openings from within.

The goal of all such programs is to assist promising employees who nonetheless lack specific skills required for advanced job positions. These programs face a dilemma: Sending employees to training classes takes them away from the jobs where they gain practical experience, credibility, and acceptance within the company. E-learning can help by providing just the training needed by each targeted individual without taking him or her off the job.

Economics of Advancing Targeted Individuals

Rapidly advancing employees can prove expensive. Here is an example. The OZ Vacuum Cleaning Company wants to advance Dotty Redshoe one managerial level. First, tally the costs that would occur without the use of e-learning.

To provide knowledge and skills normally acquired over years in the job, Dotty will need extensive training and education. The estimated cost for such training is $20,000, including registration fees and tuition in necessary courses. It also includes travel expenses while attending training at distant locations. Because the goal is to train Dotty as quickly as possible, considerable travel may be needed so she can attend the earliest available courses.

Another major cost is Dotty's salary. Say that the training requires her to be away from the job for 12 weeks. Assuming a salary of $1,500 per week (including benefits), the time costs add $18,000 to the total.

Not all training is formal. Much of the training necessary to advance a level must come from increased interaction with her supervisor and other higher-level managers. Suppose that these informal tutors and coaches make $2,000 per week and that eight weeks of coaching is needed. That adds another $16,000 to the total.

Adding up all these costs, you see that fast-tracking Dotty costs $54,000. Wonder if e-learning can help? Run the numbers again, this time assuming that e-learning is used to the maximum extent possible for delivering the needed training.

Well, because e-learning does not require travel and can be targeted quite precisely, the basic cost of training is cut in half, making it $10,000. The reduction in travel also reduces the time off the job by two-thirds, cutting it from 12 to four weeks and saving $12,000.

The use of higher quality and better targeted e-learning may reduce the time that the supervisor must spend tutoring Dotty. Some of the tutoring can be made more efficient if conducted by telementoring or e-coaching mechanisms. Assume that the amount of supervisor time can be reduced from eight weeks to six weeks, thus saving $4,000.

E-learning thus reduces the cost of advancing an employee to $28,000, a savings of $26,000. Table 3-4 summarizes this analysis. As usual, you can download the spreadsheet containing this calculation from the book's Website (www.horton.com/using) and plug in your own numbers. Why not try out different salary levels for employee and supervisor, different amounts of off-the-job time, and some variation in coaching time required.

Table 3-4. Using e-learning to advance an employee.

	Before	After	Savings	
Cost of training	$20,000	$10,000	$10,000	per employee
Employee's current salary	$1,500	$1,500	—	per week
Time off job for training	12	4	8	weeks
Cost of time off job	$18,000	$6,000	$12,000	per employee
Supervisor's salary	$2,000	$2,000	—	per week
Time required coaching	8	6	2	weeks
Cost of supervisor's time	$16,000	$12,000	$4,000	per employee
Total costs	$54,000	$28,000	$26,000	per employee

Using E-Learning to Advance Targeted Individuals

Advancing targeted individuals requires identifying the learning needs that separate them from targeted positions and crafting programs that efficiently provide what is needed. Here are some suggestions:

- ☐ Use online testing to assess and monitor the employee's skills and knowledge.
- ☐ Have "learning counselors" create a blended program based on the individual and the target job. This custom program can include e-learning courses, online reading assignments, and specified collaborative work.
- ☐ Design e-learning to be easily navigated so learners can skip what they already know and what they do not need to know.
- ☐ Give employees e-learning tuition to buy access to the publicly available courses they need.
- ☐ Use telementoring to link employees with appropriate role models and coaches.
- ☐ Institute best practices programs to capture knowledge of senior employees. Have junior employees interview, paraphrase, and record these best practices, thereby making this knowledge available for training employees and imparting it to the junior employees involved in the program.

SMOOTHING LABOR RELATIONS

Labor relations have changed considerably from the confrontational 1970s and 1980s when labor and management fought fierce battles, primarily over wages. Today the adversarial relationship continues, but cooperation is often a goal in negotiations. Today, management's primary concern may be achieving the flexibility to adapt to changing business conditions, and labor's main concern may be job security in those same changing business conditions.

Training can help meet the goals of both management and union. Training prepares workers to take on new job duties and ensures their value to the company. It also prepares them for future employment if their current employer should no longer need them. Training shows workers that their employer is willing to invest in their skills.

E-learning can reduce the time off the job required to take training or increase the amount of training that is provided in the same amount of time off the job. Two multimedia training courses for workers at Union Pacific reduced training time by 35 percent and 50 percent (Cantwell, 1993).

E-learning can demonstrate that information technology is being used to enhance productivity and improve the work environment, not just to eliminate workers. It can teach collaboration mechanisms to enhance involvement of workers in decision making.

Economics of E-Learning in Labor Relations

Here's an example of how e-learning can make training a win-win item in contract negotiations. Hoffa Cement is negotiating with its union. Currently the contract is based on 225 workdays per year, with two days allocated to training. That means that the company receives 223 days of labor per year. Management believes that each day of training increases productivity by 0.35 percent. Therefore, the current two days of training can boost productivity by 0.7 percent overall, which yields the equivalent of an additional 1.56 days of work. The investment of two days of training yields less than two days of additional production. The company is skeptical when the union asks for an additional two days of training per year. "What's this gonna cost me?" moans James Riddle, the company president.

"Perhaps nothing," says Norm Newway, the company's negotiating representative. "Suppose we agree to the two additional days of training but insist that all training be conducted by e-learning."

"How does that help?"

"We know that e-learning can be more efficient. Let's say that it adds 0.5 percent to productivity for each day of training. That means four days of training will boost productivity 2 percent. Based on 221 working days, that yields the equivalent of 4.42 additional days of work a year. Now investments in training put us in the black."

Table 3-5 summarizes this analysis. Conduct your own negotiations. Download the spreadsheet from the book's Website (www.horton.com/using), and explore the economics of labor relations. What happens if the additional training is more or less effective than assumed?

Table 3-5. E-learning makes training acceptable to management.

	Before	After	
Workdays	225	225	days
Days in training	2	4	days
Effective workdays	223	221	days
Effect on productivity	0.35%	0.50%	per day
Productivity boost	0.70%	2.00%	
Equivalent additional days	1.56	4.42	days

Using E-Learning to Smooth Labor Relations

E-learning provides lots of opportunities for win-win situations that can improve labor relations. Keep in mind that both labor and management must benefit. Otherwise, either management will not propose the idea or labor will reject it.

Also be aware that relations are full of undercurrents and subtleties. Consult with your company's labor representative and be sure to take a company labor representative to all initial meetings.

How can e-learning smooth labor relations? Here are some ideas to pursue:

- ☐ Listen to workers and their concerns first. Find out how they perceive training, what training they want, and how they prefer to get it. Get beyond your own viewpoint.
- ☐ Feature training in contract negotiations. Make clear to workers how training makes them more valuable, simplifies their work, and makes work safer and less stressful.
- ☐ Realize that any training initiative may have contract implications. Shortening a three-day training course to two days may require renegotiating over how to split the savings between the company and union workers.
- ☐ Design training programs to suit the learning abilities and styles of workers. Consider verbal skills, educational level, and computer skills. Keep in mind that many union workers may have advanced levels of job-related knowledge but not fundamental skills.

☐ Provide necessary computer skills first. In doing so, consider seniority. Those with highest seniority may have the lowest levels of computer skills.

☐ Provide facilities where workers can take e-learning close to work locations, and be sure to budget for the time. You cannot expect union workers to take training on their own time. Be realistic about the amount of time required.

◀◀ ◀◀ ◀◀ ◀◀ ◀◀ ▶▶ ▶▶ ▶▶ ▶▶ ▶▶

YOUR TURN

How can e-learning help your organization improve its operation? In this segment, consider each of the ways discussed in this chapter. Pick one and detail how e-learning can help accomplish this goal.

If you want to accomplish more than one of these objectives, good for you! Just photocopy worksheet 3-1, or download and print a copy from the book's Website (www.horton.com/using).

Worksheet 3-1. Improving organizational effectiveness.

1. Pick a General Goal

☐ Improve workforce performance
☐ Recruit and retain better employees
☐ Advance specific employees
☐ Smooth labor relations

2. Specify an Objective

Specify exactly what you hope to accomplish. Be specific. Designate specific groups of people, and spell out the percentages or amounts of improvement you anticipate for each group.

3. Identify Ways E-Learning Can Help

Specify how e-learning can help you accomplish this objective. List some specific benefits of e-learning that will directly contribute to this objective.

1. _____

2. _____

3. _____

4. Estimate the Value of the Improvement

$

5. Make Your Plan

List the exact ways you will use e-learning to achieve these benefits.

Action	Person Responsible	Due Date

4

Selling E-Learning

One way to increase the revenues of your organization is to sell e-learning products and services outside your company. These may include courses, learning modules, components, subscriptions, and custom development services. (For more on selling within your company, see the section "Becoming a Profit Center" in chapter 8.)

E-learning opens a large market for your knowledge and expertise. The World Wide Web means that you can economically offer your e-learning to the whole wide world. Furthermore, transaction costs, at least for self-directed e-learning, are low and can be largely automated.

The market for e-learning is vast. A Merrill Lynch study estimated that the market within U.S. corporations is $96 billion (Moe, 1999). The total market in the United States, including the private and public education sectors, is $740 billion. Worldwide, the market is $2 trillion. Expenditures for e-learning are expected to reach $11 billion by 2003 (Urdan & Weggen, 2000).

WHAT CAN YOU SELL?

There are many ways you can sell e-learning. You can sell both products and services. You can sell different rights to your e-learning materials. You can sell different aggregations of components as well as individual components. Take a look at the ways you can package e-learning for sale.

E-Learning Products

If a customer wants to buy e-learning content from you rather than just access to the courses, what do you offer? Consider the following:

- self-contained courses
- courses with instructions on how to facilitate them

- e-learning modules that can be assembled to form custom courses
- raw materials: hypertext mark-up language (HTML) files, graphics, multimedia components, source code.

E-Learning Services

E-learning can be sold as a service or as a collection of related services. Some of your potential service offerings are

- access to courses you host
- customization of your standard course offerings
- integration of customer content within your standard courses
- development of completely custom courses
- compilation of custom curricula
- development of custom certificate programs
- facilitation of course offerings
- e-coaching and online tutoring
- online assessment services.

Related Materials

In addition to pure e-learning, you may also market related materials. These may be materials you develop as part of your e-learning that have independent value. Candidates include the following:

- reference materials
- job aids, such as decision aids, calculators, and checklists
- handouts.

WHAT IS YOUR MARKET?

To whom do you sell your e-learning products? What organizations and individuals will pay to take or remarket your e-learning courses, modules, and components? Here are some potential external markets:

- ☐ *Users of your company's products and services:* These include those who install, operate, and customize your products.
- ☐ *Third-party trainers:* Some large technology companies, Cisco and Microsoft for example, make their training materials available to outside training companies, who rework them to add value, say by customizing them to the needs of a particular audience or localizing them to a certain country.
- ☐ *Resellers of your company's product:* These include distributors, resellers, system integrators, and value-added suppliers. They will need to bundle your training with their versions of your products.

- [ ] *Suppliers to your company:* Suppliers need to understand your requirements, your manufacturing process, your enterprise resources planning system, your quality control procedures, and your business practices and ethics. Perhaps you should have a course called, "How to Sell to Us."
- [ ] *Universities and trade schools:* Schools increasingly are looking for ways to make their academic curricula more effective in preparing students for employment. When students are preparing for jobs involving your products, they need training on those products.
- [ ] *Others in your industry:* If you have products that have become industry standards, do not overlook the need for training among those whose products must work alongside yours.

Internal markets are identified in the section of chapter 8 that deals with turning the training department into a profit center.

ECONOMICS OF SELLING E-LEARNING

Business models for e-learning are as varied as e-learning offerings. In this segment you will see two examples: one for self-directed learning and one for instructor-led e-learning. Both examples cover developing and offering the course. Though quite simple, these models do point out how profitability depends on some key assumptions.

Self-Directed E-Learning

RoboLearning, Ltd., offers learner-led e-learning courses. These courses are totally asynchronous and involve no instructor or facilitator. To delve into RoboLearning's business model, first you will calculate the projected annual profit for a single course.

Start with the revenue. For the course, assume that 1,500 learners a year will pay $100 to take the course. That yields revenue of $150,000 per year.

From these revenues you must subtract costs. Primary among these costs will be the costs of developing the course. Assume a development cost of $300,000. Such a high development cost is necessary to pay for the rich interactivity and multimedia necessary to make "instructorless" training engaging and effective. To convert this development cost to an annual cost, divide it by the service life of the course, three years in this case, to get an annualized development cost of $100,000.

To the cost of development add $20,000 to cover administrative costs, such as housing the course on a Web server, handling technical difficulties, and any other tasks that cannot be completely automated. The total costs are therefore $120,000 per year.

Profit is revenue ($150,000) minus costs ($120,000), or $30,000 per year per course. That figure represents a 20 percent profit margin—respectable but not spectacular.

Table 4-1 summarizes this analysis. Though the figures here are reasonable, they most certainly do not apply exactly to your own situation. Why not download the spreadsheet from the book's Website (www.horton.com/using) and explore the profitability from your perspective? As you do, you will discover that profitability is exquisitely sensitive to certain assumptions. For example, try reducing enrollments to 1,000 per year or extending service life to four years, instead of three.

Table 4-1. Business model for self-directed e-learning.

Revenue

Enrollments	1,500	learners per year
× Enrollment fee	$100	per learner
= Total revenue	$150,000	per year

Costs

Development cost	$300,000	per course
÷ Service life of course	3	years
= Annualized development cost	$100,000	per year
+ Administrative costs	$20,000	per year
= Total costs	$120,000	per year

Profit

Total revenue	$150,000	per year
− Total costs	$120,000	per year
= Profit	$30,000	per year
Profit margin	20%	

Instructor-Led E-Learning

The calculation of profits for instructor-led e-learning is similar in overall structure but different in the details. Look at this example: Feeling Touch Training conducts training classes over the Web. Each class, on average, draws 17 learners, each paying $150. That means each class yields $2,550 in revenue. By teaching 50 classes a year, Feeling Touch realizes $127,500 per year in revenue.

From revenue you must subtract costs. One cost is that of developing the course materials. Assume that developing this course costs $30,000. The development costs of this course are much less than the self-directed course because the live instructor will provide much of the presentation and interaction. As in the case of self-directed training, divide these costs by the service life of the course (three years) to calculate the portion of the development cost per year: $10,000 in this case.

To these costs, add the instructor's salary for the time preparing for and conducting the course, including answering emails from learners. This portion of the instructor's salary amounts to $50,000. Don't neglect the $20,000 administrative cost to pay for the costs of hosting the course on a Web server and other costs of conducting the course.

The total costs are thus $80,000, which, subtracted from the total revenues of $127,500, yields a profit of $47,500 per year—a 37 percent profit margin.

Table 4-2 summarizes this analysis. You may want to download the spreadsheet from the book's Website (www.horton.com/using) and play around with these numbers. What happens if the class size is 20, instead of 17? What if the use of streaming media requires more expensive servers? What if you conduct only 40 classes per year? What if the enrollment fee is cut to $100? What if the instructor's role is reduced to that of a facilitator?

Table 4-2. Business model for instructor-led e-learning.

Revenue

Class size	17	learners per class
× Enrollment fee	$150	per learner
= Class revenue	$2,550	per class
× Class offerings	50	classes per year
= Total revenue	$127,500	per year

Costs

Development cost	$30,000	per course
÷ Service life of course	3	years
= Annualized development cost	$10,000	per year
+ Instructor salary	$50,000	per year
+ Administrative costs	$20,000	per year
= Total costs	$80,000	per year

Profit

Total revenue	$127,500	per year
− Total costs	$80,000	per year
= Profit	$47,500	per year
Profit margin	37%	

REFINING YOUR BUSINESS MODEL

If you are going to sell e-learning, you must pick and refine your business model, which is your plan for making money. A business model for e-learning spells out from whom you buy, to whom you sell, what you buy and sell, and how much you charge and pay. Here are some of the choices you can make in assembling your business plan.

How Do You Do Business?

One of the most fundamental choices you must make is the kind of business you want to operate. How will you appear to customers? Although many forms are possible, several categories of e-learning businesses are common. These are detailed in table 4-3.

Table 4-3. Forms of e-learning businesses.

Business Form	What They Sell	How They Obtain What They Sell
Portal	Access to courses through their Website.	Contract with other course providers who may individually host their own courses. Some portals develop their own courses as well.
Applications Services Provider (ASP)	Hosting services for e-learning courses.	Customers provide content, which the ASP hosts and integrates with a learning management system and other services.
Course Supplier	Courses that customers can take from the course supplier's server or host on their own server.	Develop courses internally.
Contract Developer	Development of custom e-learning to their customers' specifications.	Develop courses internally.

What Rights Do You Sell?

When you "sell" e-learning, what exactly do buyers get? After paying you money, what are they legally entitled to do with your course or other e-learning offering? Here are some possible rights you may grant:

- take a course on your server
- host your course on their server
- resell the course

- sell access to the course
- modify and customize the course
- anything they want.

Each different set of rights will constitute a different product or service you can sell.

How Do You Price Your Products and Services?

In what units do you sell your offerings and how are you compensated? Answers to these questions constitute your pricing model. Many models are possible. Table 4-4 lists a few of the most common ones along with their main advantages and disadvantages.

Table 4-4. Pricing models for e-learning.

Model	How It Works	Advantages	Disadvantages
Ticket	You charge an entrance fee for each student enrolling in a course.	• Accounting is simple. • Revenue is proportional to enrollment. • High enrollments are quite profitable.	• A high fee may discourage browsing. • Low enrollments may fail to recover costs.
Library Card	Each learner pays a fee that grants access to a library of courses for a period of time.	• Revenue is predictable up front. • Customers like the fixed up-front cost and the fact that learners have access to more courses.	• Usage is hard to predict.
Rental	Learners pay by the hour or minute within an e-learning system; also called "pay as you go."	• Up-front price appears lower to customers because they pay for just what they use.	• Learners may resent the pressure to complete courses in the minimum amount of time.
Group Subscription	All members of the group have access to all of your courses for the period of the subscription; also called a site license.	• You receive revenues up front or at least have a predictable cash flow for the period of the subscription. • Customers like the predictable flat fee.	• Usage is not predictable.
Server-license	Companies license the right to put your course on their servers.	• You get a predictable lump of cash up front. • Your support costs are low. • Customers like the one-time fee regardless of how many they train.	• Licensing fees may be lower than revenues from other models.

How Much Do You Charge?

Setting prices for your e-learning offerings is one of the most critical business decisions you will make. Price courses too high, and enrollments will be low. Price courses too low, and you do not make enough per unit to recover your costs. No hard-and-fast rules govern pricing for e-learning offerings, but here are some factors that affect how much you can charge for your course:

■ *Competition:* What is the price being charged for analogous courses covering the same subject at the same depth? For generic courses, competition will determine prices.

■ *Timeliness:* How eager is the market for training on the subject of your e-learning? If your e-learning provides timely knowledge that is in high demand, you can charge a high price.

■ *Reputation:* Will your authority and stature among learners allow your courses to command a premium? Or, are you competing against a big name in the industry?

■ *Predilections:* Do learners prefer classroom training? If so, you must price your e-learning offerings less than comparable classroom courses.

■ *Efficiency:* If potential learners are especially busy, they may be willing to pay a premium for a course that conveys knowledge and skills in the minimum amount of time.

In setting an initial price for your course, try to view your course from the perspective of the potential buyer who may not know anything about you or your company or about how much blood, sweat, tears, and toil you have put into developing your e-learning. *The appropriate price is the amount your e-learning is worth to them, not how much it means to you.*

HOW TO SELL E-LEARNING

To sell e-learning for a profit you will need a sound business plan, a capable and talented team, adequate financing, and a few megabytes of luck. Remember these tips from people who have sold e-learning for a profit:

☐ Cater to your market. What do they need? What do they want? What will they pay for? How much will they pay?

☐ Assess your market's readiness for e-learning. Do they have the necessary infrastructure? Do they view e-learning positively?

☐ Sell everything several times. Design components so you can configure "semi-customized" courses from a library of reusable modules. Design to standards for interoperability, for example, the Sharable Content Object Reference Model (SCORM), the Aviation Industry Computer-Based

Training Committee (AICC) guidelines, and the IMS Global Learning Consortium (IMS) standards (Horton, 2001).

☐ **Control costs.** Test your business model to see which costs have the greatest effects on profitability and then take steps to minimize these costs. Are development costs more critical than delivery costs? Do infrastructure costs really matter?

☐ **Manage your cash flow.** How will you pay the up-front costs of designing, developing, and promoting courses until sales generate an adequate income stream? What if getting your e-learning to market takes longer than anticipated (and it always does)?

☐ **Engineer repeat business.** Design sequences of courses from the most basic to the most advanced so that learners can buy course after course. Consider clustering courses into certificate programs.

☐ **Tell the world.** Do not expect learners to find your courses on their own. Register with search engines. Send out mailings and email broadcasts. Take out ads on the Web and in print.

◀◀ ◀◀ ◀◀ ◀◀ ◀◀ ▶▶ ▶▶ ▶▶ ▶▶ ▶▶

YOUR TURN

If you plan to sell e-learning to raise revenues, you need a business plan. Here are the decisions you will need to make to flesh out your plan.

Step 1. Decide What You Will Offer

Your first step is to decide what you plan to sell. List your planned offerings in worksheet 4-1.

Worksheet 4-1. Products, services, and materials you will offer for sale.		
Products	**Services**	**Materials**

Step 2. Build Your Economic Model

Calculate how you will make money and how much you will make. If you plan to sell courses, you can use worksheet 4-2 to calculate profits, or you can download the spreadsheets from the book's Website (www.horton.com/using). For other offerings, you may need to use a different formula.

Worksheet 4-2. Economic model for e-learning.

Revenue

Class size		learners per class
× Offerings per year		classes per year
= Annual enrollments		learners per year
× Enrollment fee	$	per learner
= Annual revenue	$	per year

Costs

Development cost	$	per course
÷ Service life of course		years
= Annualized development cost	$	per year
+ Administrative costs	$	per year
= Total Costs	$	per year

Profit

Total revenue	$	per year
− Total costs	$	per year
= Profit	$	per year

Profit margin		%

Step 3. Pick a Form of Business

Which kind of business do you plan to operate? Pick one and briefly justify your choice. Enter your choices on worksheet 4-3.

Worksheet 4-3. Choose a type of business.	
Type of Business	**Reasons for Choosing This Form**
☐ Portal ☐ Application services provider ☐ Course supplier ☐ Contract developer ☐ Other: _____	

Step 4. Pick a Pricing Model

How do you plan to price your offerings? Pick a pricing model and justify your choice. Enter your choice on worksheet 4-4.

Worksheet 4-4. Choose a pricing model.	
Pricing Model	**Reasons for Choosing This Model**
☐ Ticket ☐ Library card ☐ Rental ☐ Group subscription ☐ Server-license ☐ Other: _____	

Step 5. Price Your Offerings

Taking into account the competition, the timeliness of your offerings, your organization's reputation, the preferences of your learners, and the efficiency of your offerings, put a price on your offerings. Use worksheet 4-5 as a guide.

Worksheet 4-5. Pricing your e-learning offerings.

First, make a rough estimate of what your e-learning offering may be worth in the marketplace:

$_____ per _____

Now, determine if you need to adjust your price upward or downward based on these factors:

E-Learning Marketplace Factor	Effect on Price of Your Offering (Up/Down)
Competition: Compare your estimated price to competitors' prices for similar services/products.	
Timeliness: Is your product or service on the leading edge and available before your competitors'?	
Reputation: Will your authority and stature among learners allow your courses to command a premium? Are you up against a big name as a competitor?	
Predilections: Do your learners prefer e-learning or classroom training?	
Efficiency: Are your learners willing to pay a premium price to acquire new skills and knowledge in less time?	
Final Price for Your E-Learning Offering	$

5

Reducing Costs of Training

Within most complex organizations, the costs of training are among the highest. The budget for the training department is only a small fraction of the total costs of training throughout an organization. These additional costs seldom show up explicitly on the organization's balance sheet because they are distributed through many departments and activities.

CAN E-LEARNING CUT TRAINING COSTS?

E-learning has proven most effective in lowering a wide range of training costs. By switching from conventional classroom training to e-learning:

- Storage Technology reduced training costs by 46 percent (Hall, 2000b).
- PricewaterhouseCoopers reduced per-student costs from $706 to $106 (Hall, 2000b).
- Training for Novell certification was reduced from $1,800 to about $800 per person (Terry, 1998).
- MCI WorldCom cut training costs $5.6 million on one project (Kroll, 1999).
- Aetna reduced the costs for training 3,000 employees by $3 million—a savings of $1,000 per employee (Kroll, 1999).
- Buckman Laboratories cut the costs of training employees to use its email system by 84 percent (Gillette, 1998).
- Cisco reduced training costs from $1,500 per person to just $120—a 92 percent reduction (Terry, 1998).

KINDS OF COSTS

E-learning can help reduce both the direct and indirect costs of training. Direct costs of training include the costs of developing and offering training. Among these are the up-front analysis and design costs, the costs of building

Caveat on Costs

Costs are treacherous and have no ethics. They sneak up on you and clobber you when you are not looking!

- Costs plot and conspire together. Lowering one cost almost inevitably raises another. Anything you do to lower development costs, for example, is almost certain to increase delivery costs.
- One person's cost is another person's benefit. Remember to analyze costs from multiple perspectives: that of the person developing the training, the person selling the training, the person buying it, and the person taking it. What is an outrageous cost to one may be an entitlement to another.
- Some costs are more evil than others. Focus on the costs that matter most. Pay special attention to costs that you pay, ones that limit your success, ones that are the biggest, and ones that threaten relationships with your customers.

or otherwise acquiring courses, and the costs of delivering the courses. Delivery costs include the salaries of instructors and the costs of classroom facilities. To these costs, which are borne by the training department, must be added the costs paid by the trainee's organization, the most important of which are the costs of travel to take training.

Indirect costs include some that are just as important even though they are less visible. Large among these indirect costs are the time employees spend in training and the cost of work that does not get done while they are away from their jobs. Another indirect training cost is the time that supervisors, managers, and co-workers spend informally coaching employees who lack needed skills and knowledge.

The sections that follow consider each of these costs in turn and how e-learning can be used to reduce them.

DELIVERY COSTS

Delivery costs are the costs of offering training once it has been developed. These are the costs paid each time you conduct training. These costs can mount up when you are training many people over a long period of time.

Delivery costs commonly include the salaries of instructors and facilitators, their travel costs, costs of printing and binding handouts, textbooks, refreshments and meals, shipping of materials to the site of training, and the administrative costs of registering and tracking learners. Delivery costs do not include travel costs of learners or the costs of classroom buildings and equipment. These costs are covered later in this chapter.

How E-Learning Can Help

E-learning can reduce or eliminate many of the delivery costs required for classroom instruction.

By removing the requirement for the instructor to travel to the site of training, e-learning eliminates instructor time lost in travel and recovering from jet lag. For example, Ilya Zaslavsky, an assistant professor at Western Michigan University in Kalamazoo, Michigan, was able to conduct his geography classes while on leave in San Diego (Microsoft Corporation, 1998a). A facilitated e-learning course may require less direct time of the instructor. A self-directed e-learning course may not require an instructor at all.

E-learning also reduces costs for paper, printing, and binding, or at least it passes these costs on to the learner. Electronically prepared materials can be downloaded, viewed on the screen, and printed locally by learners. Not only does e-learning reduce printing, it also eliminates the need to ship cartons of handouts and other materials to the location of training.

E-learners seem perfectly content to supply their own coffee, doughnuts, pencils, pads of paper, and other incidentals.

And, with e-learning, much of the administration can be automated. Students can register themselves, the system can track their completion of modules, and diplomas can be automatically generated.

Economics of Delivering Learning

Explore the economics of delivering learning. William Nelson, CEO of On The Road Training, is concerned that the costs of delivering training classes is higher than it need be and undertakes an analysis of alternatives. Table 5-1 compares the delivery costs for a traditional instructor-led class, for facilitated e-learning, and for self-directed e-learning. The costs are those for teaching a two-day class of about 15 to 20 learners at a location to which the instructor must travel (for the instructor-led class).

One of the main costs is the instructor's time. For the classroom version, the instructor must spend two days teaching, a day traveling to the site, and a day returning. For facilitated e-learning, the instructor's teaching time is only one and one-half days because the instructor does not have to present material directly. And there is no travel. Assuming an instructor's salary of $400 per day (including benefits), the cost of the instructor's time is $1,600 for classroom training and $600 for facilitated e-learning. For self-directed e-learning, there is no instructor, hence no instructor costs.

For the classroom version, On the Road Training must pay the travel costs (airfare, hotel, taxi, meals, and so forth) for the instructor. These costs average $1,500 per class. Other costs for classroom training include printing and binding handouts ($400), shipping handouts and other materials to the site of training ($100), and refreshments and meals ($200). Neither form of e-learning entails any of these travel or other costs.

The final category of delivery costs consists of the administrative costs of registering students, printing up name tents and tags, recording their completion of the course, and generating diplomas and certificates. For the classroom version, assume this work takes one day of an administrator's time. At a salary rate of $250 per day, the cost of administrative work is $250 per class.

For e-learning, much of the administration can be automated by systems that allow self-registration, automatic tracking of test scores, and screen-displayed diplomas that students can print out on their own. Some human administration is required, but only a tenth of a day. Therefore, the administrative costs for either form of e-learning are only $25.

The total costs are thus $4,050 for instructor-led classroom training, $625 for facilitated e-learning, and $25 for self-directed e-learning. E-learning excels in lowering delivery costs. But, don't count your benefits yet. These lowered delivery costs may be offset by increases in other costs. Read on.

Table 5-1 summarizes this analysis. Why not download the spreadsheet from the book's Website (www.horton.com/using) and see what the savings would be in your case. Or, try some experiments such as making the facilitated e-learning more like self-directed or more like instructor-led classroom training.

Table 5-1. Costs of three ways of delivering training.

	Instructor-Led Classroom Training	Facilitated E-Learning	Self-Directed E-Learning	
Instructor's time teaching	2	1.5	0	days per class
+ Instructor's travel time	2	0	0	days per class
= Instructor's time	4.0	1.5	0.0	days per class
× Instructor's salary	$400	$400	$400	per day
= Cost of instructor's time	$1,600	$600	$0	per class
Instructor's travel	$1,500	$0	$0	per class
Printing and binding handouts	$400	$0	$0	per class
Shipping	$100	$0	$0	per class
Refreshments and meals	$200	$0	$0	per class
Administration time	1.0	0.1	0.1	days per class
× Administrator's salary	$250	$250	$250	per day
= Cost of administration time	$250	$25	$25	per class
Total costs	$4,050	$625	$25	per class

Using E-Learning to Lower Delivery Costs

If your goal is to reduce delivery costs of training, use e-learning to eliminate or reduce common costs of delivering training. Consider these alternatives:

☐ Use self-directed e-learning if practical. Otherwise, use lightly facilitated e-learning rather than instructor-led e-learning.

- [ ] Replace printed materials with online materials that learners can download, view on the screen, and print out as necessary.
- [ ] Invest in a sophisticated learning management system to automate administrative activities such as registration, tracking, reporting, and record keeping. (Note: Such a system may increase facility costs.)
- [ ] Enable facilitators or online instructors to work from any location, even their homes.

Initial E-Learning May Increase Delivery Costs

Some instructors report that electronic delivery requires 40 to 50 percent more effort on their parts (Brown, 1998). Students, lacking face-to-face contact, demand more attention and feedback from instructors. Some instructors felt they had become, in effect, private tutors (Iadevaia, 1999).

Often learners report that e-learning courses take 20 to 40 percent more time and effort than traditional classroom courses (Kroder, Suess & Sachs, 1998). Online discussions, brainstorming sessions, and problem-solving activities may take longer than their face-to-face counterparts (Moore, 1995). Lacking the feedback of facial expressions, body language, and tone of voice, participants in online communications must spend more time apologizing for unintended insults, correcting misinterpretations, and clarifying ambiguities and less time on the matter of the discussion.

These negative results are not universal and may represent the normal inefficiency of initial efforts at e-learning. Be cautious, however, about promising high efficiency for your first e-learning efforts.

DEVELOPMENT COSTS

Development costs are those required to prepare materials to the point where a course can be offered to learners. These costs include:

- planning learning activities and instructional sequences
- writing tests and other assessments
- locating appropriate examples and case studies
- creating visual displays and other media elements
- scripting narration and commentary
- preparing answers for anticipated questions.

For instructor-led courses, development may include training the instructors who will go forth and conduct courses at distant locations. For e-learning, development often includes designing and creating extensive multimedia components and programming rich interactivity.

How E-Learning Can Help

It can't. How's that for blunt honesty? According to testimony by the American Federation of Teachers before the Web-based Education Commission, creating e-learning courses can take 66 to 500 percent longer than for traditional class-room courses (Web-Based Education Commission, 2000).

The thrust of the discussion here will be on how much of a premium orga-nizations must pay to develop e-learning courses and ways to keep e-learning development costs to a minimum. Both of these are crucial topics as develop-ment costs are likely to be the largest budget item on an e-learning project.

Reality Check

I have been involved in network-based training for more than 30 years and know of no example where developing true e-learning was less expensive than developing traditional classroom training. Every claim I have investigated fell apart when I began adding in hidden costs or those just shifted to other departments.

Of course, development costs depend on many factors such as the complexity of the material, how much of it already exists in electronic form, how much interactivity and multimedia you need to use, and whether there will be a live facilitator to get learners out of trouble. Costs for self-directed e-learning based on valid instructional design can range up to $25,000 (Bork, 1997) or even $60,000 (Becker, 1999) per hour of instruction. I have seen labor esti-mates of 50 to 200 hours of work for each hour of e-learning created from scratch and 10 to 50 hours per hour of e-learning created by converting an instructionally sound classroom course. As a rule, developing technology-based training costs three to four times as much as developing conventional classroom training (Allen, 1999).

Yet, I have also seen estimates of $500 per hour of e-learning! Just keep in mind that it takes no special effort or talent to shove some PowerPoint slides on a Web server and call them "e-learning." Unfortunately, the amount of learning that takes place is much harder to measure than the length of time the purported learner sits in front of the computer. *Caveat emptor.*

W.H.

Economics of E-Learning Development

Here is an example of the kinds of development costs you may encounter while developing training.

Tryphrenic Train, an imaginary purveyor of didactic delights, is considering three forms of training for its next offering. Table 5-2 shows Tryphrenic's anal-ysis. It compares the costs of developing one hour of training for instructor-led classroom training, for facilitated e-learning, and for self-directed e-learning. "One hour of training" means the amount of learning that takes place during one hour of classroom training designed by a competent designer and taught by a competent instructor. The "hour" may require only 45 minutes of seat time in e-learning, or it may require 90 minutes. It is the amount of learning that is constant across all three cases.

This analysis divides costs into three phases of development. The first phase, research and design, covers researching the subject matter and the intended learners and then specifying the necessary learning experiences. For the three forms of training, the times required are 30, 40, and 50 hours. Although the time required to research the subject and learners is the same in all three cases, e-learning will require a more careful instructional design because fewer successful models exist and because the e-learning designer must understand the effects of technologies used. The design for self-directed e-learning must be especially rigorous as there will be no human to answer questions or correct misconceptions.

The time rates for e-learning designers are likewise higher than for conventional classroom trainers. E-learning is new; experienced, successful designers are in short supply. For conventional training, research and design costs $50 per hour whereas for e-learning it may be $70 per hour. The result is that research costs increase progressively as you move from classroom to e-learning: $1,500, $2,800, and $3,500 for the three forms.

The next group of costs are those for media creation. For classroom training, media may include PowerPoint slides, workbooks, and paper tests. For e-learning, media include multimedia presentations, simulations, discussion forums, chat sessions, online tests, and other electronic media. The hours required for the three forms are 15, 80, and 120 hours, respectively. E-learning requires more electronic media and more sophisticated forms of electronic media. Self-directed e-learning requires more than facilitated e-learning because all explanations must be self-contained, and all assessments must be automatically scored. The time rates for creating traditional classroom media are about $50 per hour, but for e-learning they are upwards of $120 per hour.

For e-learning, you may need advanced multimedia developers and programmers, many of whom will be hired on a consulting basis at expectedly high consulting rates. The resulting media development costs show a sharp incline as you move from conventional classroom training to self-directed e-learning: $750, $9,600, and $14,400 per hour of instruction. Clearly, media creation costs are a substantial part of the costs of developing any form of e-learning.

A final group of costs are those for integration. This rather vague term includes all the activities required to put the components together into a working course. For classroom training, integration includes training and rehearsing the trainers. For e-learning, it includes linking together the various software packages and components, testing and refining materials, validating online tests, and debugging simulations and other online activities. It should come as no surprise that integration takes longer for e-learning and longest for self-directed e-learning, which relies on more technology to do everything. Time estimates are 15, 30, and 50 hours respectively. And, it is not surprising too that the time rates are higher along the same profile: $50, $60, and $70 per hour. The resulting totals are $750 for instructor-led classroom training, $1,800 for facilitated e-learning, and $3,500 for self-directed e-learning. Tallying these costs yields totals for each hour of instruction: $3,000 for instructor-led classroom training, $14,200 for facilitated e-learning, and $21,400 for self-directed e-learning. Table 5.2 summarizes this analysis.

Table 5-2. Development costs for three forms of training.

	Instructor-Led Classroom Training	Facilitated E-Learning	Self-Directed E-Learning	
Research and design	30	40	50	hours
× Time rate	$50	$70	$70	per hour
= Research and design cost	$1,500	$2,800	$3,500	
Media creation	15	80	120	hours
× Time rate	$50	$120	$120	per hour
= Media creation costs	$750	$9,600	$14,400	
Integration	15	30	50	hours
× Time rate	$50	$60	$70	per hour
= Integration costs	$750	$1,800	$3,500	
Total costs	$3,000	$14,200	$21,400	

Before You Scan in That Dilbert Cartoon

One drawback of e-learning is that instructors are required to obtain a license to use works in e-learning that they could use freely in the classroom under the fair use provisions of copyright law. So, before you scan in that cartoon, rip that tune, or copy that icon, make sure you have permission to use it online. Budget the time and money to obtain permission—or find substitutes for copyrighted works.

If you think these assumptions are off base, or you would just like to try some variations, please do so. Just download the spreadsheet from the companion Website (www.horton.com /using). You may want to experiment by computing development costs for a fourth option: Web-conducted classroom courses where the instructor actively presents information and presides over online meetings.

Reducing Development Costs for E-Learning

To hold development costs for e-learning in check, pick forms of e-learning that require less development, streamline your development process, and use easily created media. Here are some tips:

☐ Don't try to teach everything. Focus the course on primary objectives. Teach the most important ideas, and then link to online reference materials where learners can study related information on their own.

☐ Buy, license, rent, or borrow courses or components that can meet all or part of your training needs. By doing so you share the development costs with other organizations.

- [ ] Develop and purchase learning modules so you can inexpensively assemble courses from existing modules. Consider investing in a standards-compliant learning management system.
- [ ] Reuse existing content such as online reports, brochures, data sheets, product descriptions, and other materials. Supplement such information components with interactive practices and assessments.
- [ ] Use human instructors. Instead of expensive multimedia, rely on human-human interaction. Style online offerings as seminars with rich discussions among participants.
- [ ] Develop templates, models, frameworks, and other tools that can streamline your production work flow. License libraries of clip art and other reusable media.
- [ ] Develop courses in batches that share common navigation schemes, templates, and underlying software.
- [ ] Subcontract out work you cannot do economically. Be sure to specify precisely what you want done so there is little rework required.

INFRASTRUCTURE COSTS

Infrastructure refers to the expensive items that are shared across many courses. For conventional classroom training, this category includes the costs of building and maintaining classrooms, break rooms, and administrative offices. Infrastructure can include equipment within buildings as well: projectors, computers, whiteboards, easel pads, chairs, tables, desks, pointers, and so forth. Infrastructure costs may also include the salaries of janitors, electricians, plumbers, and technicians who keep training facilities operational.

For e-learning, some physical buildings may be necessary, but most e-learning infrastructure is electronic and network-based. E-learning infrastructure includes the costs of purchasing, setting up, and running the servers needed to host e-learning courses, stream dynamic media, and host online meetings and conversations. E-learning infrastructure may also include the computers on which e-learners take e-learning and the network over which such courses are accessed, though only a portion of these costs can rightly be attributed to e-learning.

Infrastructure costs are notoriously difficult to identify and track accurately. Many of them are long-term costs buried in capital appropriation budgets. Often they are shared among so many different training and nontraining projects that it is impossible to apportion them to a specific course or other unit of training. The training department often ignores infrastructure costs not paid by consumers of training or by another department. Often it is easier to reduce infrastructure costs than it is to calculate them.

How E-Learning Can Help

E-learning can reduce infrastructure costs for training whenever virtual, electronic facilities are less expensive than the physical facilities required for conventional training. Kent State University, working with IBM and ILINC, built a distributed learning network that enabled Kent State to increase enrollment by 30 percent without adding additional buildings (Maher, 1998). Such results are usually the case when e-learning can be conducted using existing intranets, desktop computers, and Internet connections.

Economics of Infrastructure Costs

Over the next several years, Thundering Hoard, Inc., needs to train 20,000 employees a year. To do so will require setting up a training center of 10 classrooms and 20 private offices. How much will such a training center cost? Would e-learning lower facility costs? In computing infrastructure costs, Thundering Hoard wants to consider all infrastructure costs, not just those borne directly by the training department.

Table 5-3 shows the results of the analysis. It shows the infrastructure costs per year for the required training center and infrastructure costs for performing the same amount of training by e-learning.

From commercial real estate listings, Thundering Hoard determines that the annual lease for the floor space needed for classrooms and offices would be $600,000 and $200,000, respectively. In addition, the annualized costs of equipment and furniture would be $5,000 per classroom and $1,000 per office or $70,000 total. To this would be added a $100,000 cost of maintenance. Because the training to be performed is not computer related, no computers are required in the training center. The total annual cost of infrastructure is $970,000 per year.

For facilitated e-learning, the physical infrastructure is slight, but the electronic infrastructure is substantial. Facilitated e-learning requires office space for the facilitator ($10,000), some equipment ($1,000), and a bit of routine maintenance ($1,000). Because facilitated e-learning requires servers for hosting the course and conducting collaborative activities, a cost of $10,000 is assumed for servers.

Upgrading the computers needed by 20,000 learners is estimated to cost $1 million. Because such costs are often borne by users or their departments, you can see why such costs are often ignored in computing infrastructure costs.

Thundering Hoard's intranet is currently adequate to access e-learning so that cost remains zero. The company must, however, include the costs of software required for e-learning. In this case, $100,000 per year is budgeted for a learning management system and $50,000 for collaboration software.

Adding up the costs of infrastructure needed for facilitated e-learning yields a total of $1.172 million, 21 percent more than for classroom training.

For self-directed e-learning, infrastructure costs are fewer than for facilitated e-learning. No facilitator, office space, equipment, or maintenance is required. Because self-directed e-learning does not involve extensive collaboration, no collaboration server or software is required. That means that the cost for servers is just $5,000. The costs of upgrading learners' computers and of the learning management system are the same as for facilitated e-learning. The resulting total is $1.105 million, between the costs of the other two alternatives. Table 5-3 summarizes this analysis.

Table 5-3. Calculating infrastructure costs.

	Instructor-Led Classroom Training	Facilitated E-Learning	Self-Directed E-Learning
Classrooms	$600,000	$0	$0
Offices	$200,000	$10,000	$0
Equipment and furniture	$70,000	$1,000	$0
Maintenance	$100,000	$1,000	$0
Servers	$0	$10,000	$5,000
Users' computers	$0	$1,000,000	$1,000,000
Network	$0	$0	$0
Learning management system	$0	$100,000	$100,000
Collaboration software	$0	$50,000	$0
Total	$970,000	$1,172,000	$1,105,000

Not happy that e-learning infrastructure costs are higher or that network costs were ignored? Why not download the spreadsheet from the companion Website (www.horton.com/using) and make any changes you feel necessary. Use the spreadsheet to answer these questions: What would infrastructure costs be if e-learning did not require upgrading learner's computers? What would infrastructure costs be in a company that had no intranet or desktop computers? What if classrooms had to contain computers for each student? What would infrastructure costs be for your situation?

Using E-Learning to Reduce Infrastructure Costs

To keep infrastructure costs for e-learning to a minimum, consider these suggestions:

☐ Design and buy e-learning that runs on the computers users already have and over networks already in place.

☐ Where possible, obtain e-learning through portals or have application service providers host your courses. Let someone else pay for the e-infrastructure of hosting courses.

☐ Use self-directed e-learning, which requires less software and fewer offices and other physical facilities.

☐ If eliminating the familiar structure of classroom training would prove too traumatic for learners or instructors, set up virtual facilities with electronic analogues for whiteboards, raised hands for asking questions, student lounges, and so forth.

☐ Let online facilitators and instructors work from their offices instead of from a classroom or studio.

☐ Shop around to compare prices of expensive software packages. For example, as of November 2001 there were more than 50 learning management systems. Competition will inevitably lower prices, and the need for the competitors to differentiate their offerings will ensure that there are products in all price ranges.

☐ Do not buy more than you need. If you only have 1,000 learners, you do not need a collaboration tool that handles hundreds of thousands.

Free Advice and Worth the Price

Some training departments are real estate empires in disguise. Be careful when you suggest dismantling an empire. I once had the director of the largest training center for a multinational company tell me that he agreed that e-learning was in the best interest of his company but would oppose it anyway because it would lead to a reduction in his operations. Before you tell someone that you are going to eliminate their job or what they love about it, tell them how you are going to create a better job for them.

W.H.

TRAVEL COSTS

For many companies, travel is one of the largest costs of training. Among U.S. corporations, up to 40 percent of the cost of corporate training is for employees to travel to the site of training (Becker, 1999). Travel also contributes to stress. In fact, a quarter of business professionals said that business travel was a significant source of stress (Crookston, 1999).

Many organizations are using e-learning as the axe to fell out-of-control travel costs associated with training. Aetna estimated that for training 1,200 employees, travel expenses would cost $5 million—$4,166 per person (Kroll, 1999). The first year of Eli Lilly & Company's Web-based training program saved the company $800,000 in travel and salary costs over classroom training (McGee, 1998).

If travel costs are a large component of your organization's training expenses, start deploying e-learning soon, because it can eliminate travel requirements or at least minimize them.

Economics of Travel for Training

Table 5-4 shows a typical expense report for a person who must fly from Boston to Denver to take a two-day training class.

Table 5-4. Typical expense report for a two-day training class.

Taxi to airport	$30
Airfare	$800
Rental car	$150
Lodging	$250
Meals	$125
Telephone charges	$10
Tips and other minor items	$25
Taxi home from airport	$30
Total	$1,420

To calculate the potential savings by using e-learning instead, multiply this total by the number of learners who must travel to take training.

Using E-Learning to Reduce Travel Costs

Identify courses that have the highest travel expenses. Look for courses needed internationally but which foreign employees cannot take because of travel. Also look for short courses for which the class length cannot justify travel. Among these courses, which ones can be easily taught by e-learning?

If you do not have time or budget to immediately develop complete, pure e-learning, consider these compromises:

- [ ] Design concise e-learning courses covering the essentials of the subject to help learners get by until in-depth training is available in e-learning.
- [ ] Webcast classroom courses so that distant learners can sit in electronically.
- [ ] For generic subjects, give distant learners "tuition assistance" that they can use to buy training from portals or other sources of e-learning.

Travel Is Not Just an Expense

To some, travel is not an expense. It is a benefit. Some learners may perceive traveling for training as a company-paid vacation, especially if it takes them out of a cold, wet, dreary winter landscape, lodges them in a luxury hotel, and leaves them free time to explore an interesting location.

Also consider the social benefits of congregating with others from distant parts of the same organization or others with the same general job goals. These benefits may outweigh the costs of travel to the site of training.

OPPORTUNITY COSTS

Time spent in training is time not spent doing one's job. Fears of losing work time often discourage supervisors from sending their employees for needed training. The costs of time off the job are usually accounted for by including the learner's salary in the calculation, but this figure often understates the real costs of having the employee off the job.

The real costs of time off the job are termed *opportunity costs*—the hidden costs or lost revenue that occur when critical and profitable work does not get done. By recovering these costs, sales representatives can sell more products; doctors, lawyers, engineers, consultants, and other professionals can bill more hours; and executives can negotiate more profitable business deals. Though often not accounted for, these are among the largest costs of training.

Opportunity costs pose a dilemma for many managers, professionals, and sales representatives. For example, when sales representatives (and others involved in promoting sales) are not actively selling products, sales decline. Their managers are, therefore, reluctant to take them off the job for training. Also, because many crucial employees make much of their income from sales commissions and performance-based bonuses, they are reluctant to take time off their jobs to take training. But, without training on the latest products and sales techniques, these employees may not be as valuable to the companies that employ them. The same dilemma applies to lawyers, doctors, engineers, consultants, and others who lose billable hours when they take training.

How E-Learning Can Help

E-learning helps recover opportunity costs by reducing the time off the job for training. Boeing found that its e-learning efforts allowed its 300 process designers to focus on their jobs rather than participating in classroom training (Porter, 1999). Sun Microsystems cut the time participants in sales training had to spend away from their jobs by 80 percent (Densford, 1998). Intel reduced technicians' time off the job from a maximum of 12 hours per technician to a maximum of just two hours (Hall, 2000b).

With e-learning, travel time is eliminated. Learners do not have to drive to the airport, fly to the site of training, get a rental car, navigate to the site of training, find a parking place, locate the training room, and wait for the training to begin. In e-learning, more of the learner's time is spent learning.

Well-designed e-learning lets learners customize training to their individual needs. No more sitting through a three-day class to get 15 minutes' worth of information or to get the answer to one question. ASK International replaced a weeklong classroom course providing product knowledge to sales representatives with a six-hour course made up of self-paced materials and an on-site workshop. The costs dropped from $2,500 per learner to $500 (ASK International, 1998).

E-learning can teach more efficiently. Several studies found that well-designed multimedia training could teach 30 to 50 percent faster than classroom training (Allen, 1999; Fletcher, 1990; Hall, 1999).

Employees may be willing to take some e-learning on their own time. Ford, American Airlines, and Delta Airlines gave their employees computers and network connections with this very idea in mind.

Economics of Opportunity Costs

Look at an example of using e-learning to recover opportunity costs. Wilhelmina Loman, vice president of sales for Miller Enterprises, agonizes over the need to train her company's salesforce to begin selling a new product line. She knows that when sales representatives are not in the field, sales drop from an average of $20,000 to $10,000 per sales territory. At a profit margin of 22 percent, the company loses $2,200 for each day a sales representative is not in the field. With 100 sales representatives, the potential loss is $220,000 for each day they are not in the field.

Wilhelmina plans to use e-learning to reduce the time sales representatives must be off the job. Because e-learning does not require travel and can be taken among other work duties, Wilhelmina believes e-learning can cut the number of days off for training from four to two. This savings of two days represents monetary benefit of $440,000. From this figure, she subtracts the cost of providing the e-learning, assumed to be $300,000, to calculate a net benefit of $140,000.

Table 5-5 summarizes this analysis. Perhaps you would like to see how opportunity costs affect profits in a different field. Help yourself. Just download the spreadsheet from the book's Website (www.horton.com/using), and modify it to describe a different field. Or, try some experiments with this model; change the profit margin or the time saved by using e-learning.

> ### If You Do Not Account for Opportunity Costs
>
> Rounding up the necessary data to calculate opportunity costs can be complex and expensive. If you choose not to account for the opportunity costs of your training, do at least consider the costs of employees' time while in training. In industry and government, 90 percent of learners are paid for the time they spend learning (*Training* Magazine Staff, 1999).

Table 5-5. Using e-learning to recover opportunity costs.

Average sales per territory	$20,000	per day
× Amount from sales rep	50%	depend on sales rep
= Average sales by sales rep	$10,000	per day
× Profit margin	22%	
= Profit per sales rep	$2,200	per sales rep per day
× Number of sales reps	100	sales reps
= Profit lost when reps out of field	$220,000	per day
Time off job for classroom training	4	days
− Time off job for e-learning	2	days
= Time saved	2	days
Opportunity costs recovered	$440,000	
− Cost of e-learning program	$300,000	
= Net benefit	$140,000	

Using E-Learning to Cut Opportunity Costs

The key to recovering opportunity costs is to keep highly leveraged workers performing the activities by which the company derives profits. The best way to do this in e-learning is to design it so as to minimize the time off the job required to take training. For example:

☐ Minimize required live events. Record presentations and briefings so learners can play them back at their convenience.

☐ Equip courses with a rich navigation scheme so learners can find the parts of the course they really need. Include a menu, index, course map, and search facility.

☐ Design small, self-directed modules that fit into a busy schedule. Try to design lessons that learners can complete in 20 to 40 minutes.

☐ Encourage learners to build learning time into their day. They may find it easier to schedule an hour a day for three weeks than to try to spend two whole days taking a course.

☐ Do not discourage people from dropping out of e-learning if it does not meet their needs. Better they get back to work than waste time learning nothing.

☐ Give employees sanction to take e-learning at their desks during work hours.

☐ Make clear that it is okay to ignore phone calls, email messages, and other potential interruptions for a couple hours a day.

☐ Encourage employees to take e-learning on their own time. Give them incentives to do so—free home computers and Internet connections, for example.

COSTS OF INFORMAL COACHING

Much training is informal training on the job by the learner's boss or a co-worker. Though valuable for social purposes and popular among learners, such "water-cooler" training is highly inefficient and may be dangerous. This method of training essentially requires a one-to-one instructor to learner ratio. And, that instructor may be a valuable specialist or manager. Time spent coaching a subordinate or co-worker is time taken away from the job by both coach and learner.

Another problem can arise if the coach is not truly knowledgeable or is not an effective and efficient teacher. The learner may come away from the exchange with misunderstandings that could endanger life, limb, and project deadlines. Such training has no quality controls, no tracking of results, and no accounting of costs or accountability for results.

E-learning can often substitute for at least part of such informal coaching. It can be taken in the workplace in small bites over a period of time. And, e-learning can provide consistency, accountability, and quality control.

Economics of Informal Coaching

Lombardi Ironworks is concerned about time consumed in informal coaching. To analyze such costs, the company commissioned the study summarized in table 5-6. It shows the costs of the coaching required by a single staff member. The three rows record the coaching time occupied by three people. The first is the employee who receives coaching. This employee receives a half-hour of coaching a day. The next two rows account for the time of the people providing the coaching, 15 minutes each from a co-worker and the employee's supervisor. To convert these to financial costs, multiply them by the labor costs of these people. Use rates of $35 for the staff and $50 for the supervisor. Multiplying these rates by the times required and totaling the results shows that informal coaching costs $38.75 per staff member per day. Multiplying that by 250 workdays per year shows that coaching costs are $9,687.50 per year, a significant but hidden cost.

Table 5-6. Costs of informal coaching.

	Time (Hours Per Day)	× Rate ($ Per Hour)	= Cost ($)
Employee receiving coaching	0.50	$35	$17.50
Co-worker offering coaching	0.25	$35	$8.75
Supervisor offering coaching	0.25	$50	$12.50
Total	1.00		$38.75
Per year	250 workdays		$9,687.50

Feel free to try out some different assumptions using the spreadsheet that you can download from the book's Website (www.horton.com/using). What if the employee requires more coaching from co-workers but less from the supervisor? What if the opposite is true? What if you were considering ultra-expensive professionals?

Using E-Learning to Reduce Informal Coaching Costs

Informal coaching is good for team bonding and succession planning. Furthermore, the advice given in coaching is usually quite specific to the problem at hand. The learner can ask questions to target needs. It is hard for e-learning to be as specific.

E-learning can make sure informal coaching is not used where not appropriate, and it can ensure that informal coaching is as efficient as possible. Here are some suggestions:

- ☐ Design small modules of training that address specific job-related issues. Create a file of frequently asked questions (FAQs) that delivers training nuggets to answer common questions.
- ☐ Tell supervisors what e-learning resources are available and encourage them to refer their staff members who need training.
- ☐ Train supervisors to make them efficient and effective coaches.
- ☐ Set up a best-practices database (or just a work-related FAQ file). Ask supervisors to have employees summarize their coaching sessions as an entry in the database.
- ☐ Establish a discussion forum with threads for different job duties.
- ☐ Use collaborative technologies to implement a telementoring or e-coaching program. Allow workers to find the best coach in the world, not just the best one around the water cooler.

◄◄ ◄◄ ◄◄ ◄◄ ◄◄ ►► ►► ►► ►► ►►

YOUR TURN

Now it is time for you to begin cutting costs. In this section, you can plan how to use e-learning to reduce costs associated with training. For each of the major cost areas in this chapter, state how you will use e-learning to reduce costs and estimate how much you can save.

Delivery Costs

How can you use e-learning to reduce delivery costs? List some specific ways you can reduce delivery costs.

        How much will these steps save you? Calculate the potential savings, using worksheet 5-1.

Worksheet 5-1. Calculating savings of delivery costs.

How much does it cost to deliver training by conventional means?	$	per learner per course
— How much would it cost to deliver training by e-learning?	$	per learner per course
= Individual savings		per learner per course
× Number of learners who could take e-learning		learners
= Estimated savings	$	per course

Development Costs

Development costs are usually higher for e-learning than for classroom training, but you can take steps to keep e-learning development costs in line. What will you do to hold down development costs for your e-learning?

How will these costs compare with those for classroom training? Use worksheet 5-2 to enter your answers.

Worksheet 5-2. Comparing development costs for classroom training and e-learning.		
Development costs for classroom training	$	per _____ (unit)
− Development costs for e-learning training	$	per _____ (unit)
Difference (amount)	$	per _____ (unit)
Difference (percentage)		%

Infrastructure Costs

Estimate the savings of using more e-learning in your training blend. Be sure to convert costs to a common basis, such as the costs to teach an equivalent number of people over the same period of time. Enter your answers on worksheet 5-3.

Infrastructure Cost	Before	After
Classrooms	$	$
Offices	$	$
Equipment and furniture	$	$
Servers	$	$
Learners' computers	$	$
Network	$	$
Learning management system	$	$
Collaboration software	$	$
Total	$	$
Savings	$	

Worksheet 5-3. Reducing infrastructure costs.

Travel Costs

How can e-learning reduce travel costs incurred for training? First, estimate the typical costs for an employee who must travel to take training. Enter your answers on worksheet 5-4.

Next, estimate how e-learning will reduce the number of people who travel to training. To calculate potential savings in travel costs, multiply this number by the travel cost per employee. Use worksheet 5-5 to perform your calculations.

Worksheet 5-4. Estimating travel costs.

Travel Cost	Amount
Transportation to and from airport	$
Airfare	$
Rental car	$
Lodging	$
Meals	$
Telephone charges	$
Taxi	$
Parking	$
Tips and other minor items	$
Other:	$
Other:	$
Other:	$
Travel Cost Per Learner	$

Worksheet 5-5. Estimating total travel-cost savings.

Number who must travel to training now	
— Number who will travel once e-learning is deployed	
= Reduction in number who travel to training	
× Travel cost per employee	$
= Savings in travel costs	$

Opportunity Costs

Identify a group within your organization that may be undertrained because of the high cost of taking these people off the job.

Group:

Estimate the cost to your organization for each day one of these workers is not on the job and also the potential savings from using e-learning to reduce the time off the job. Enter your answers on worksheet 5-6.

Worksheet 5-6. Estimating savings of opportunity costs.

Time off the job required for training now	days
− Time off the job required for training with e-learning	days
= Savings in time off the job	days
× Cost per day off the job	$
= Savings per person in the group	$
× Number of persons in the group	
= Total savings	$

How will you design and deploy e-learning to reduce opportunity costs for this group?

Costs of Informal Coaching

How much time does your organization spend on unplanned, informal coaching ("water-cooler" training)? Use worksheet 5-7 to estimate the percentage of time spent in informal training.

Worksheet 5-7. Estimating time required for informal coaching.

How much of an employee's time is spent receiving such training?	%
How much of an employee's time is spent providing such training to co-workers?	%
How much of managers' and supervisors' time is spent informally coaching employees?	%

Are these amounts excessive? If so, how can you use e-learning to reduce them to desired levels?

Section III:
Improving the Reach and
Quality of Training

E-learning can increase the effectiveness with which training accomplishes its mission. This section considers ways that you can use e-learning to improve the reach and quality of training. With e-learning, you can accomplish the following:

- Provide better training to those not adequately or economically served by current forms of training. These include those too busy for conventional training, those in distant locations, and those with common disabilities.
- Achieve common training objectives, such as getting learners started in a new field, turning novices into experts, cultivating independent learners, and increasing the effects of training back on the job.

6

Making Training Available to More People

The real value of e-learning may not be in serving people already well served by classroom training but rather in making training available to people who are not able to take classroom training or choose not to. E-learning has proven its ability to deliver training widely. More than 40,000 Boeing employees have completed e-learning courses (Porter, 1999), and 80 percent of Cisco sales staff routinely use e-learning (Hall, 2000a). To use e-learning to reach neglected groups will require designing it to meet their needs and to fit within the constraints of their lives and work habits.

WHY MAKE LEARNING MORE WIDELY AVAILABLE?

If you sell learning products and services, making training available to more people enlarges your market. Making training available to neglected groups distinguishes your offerings and can give you a competitive advantage.

If you buy or create learning products and services for the employees of your company, there are several compelling reasons to make training available to all employees. Doing so maximizes the potential of your workforce. By delivering consistent training across the company, you ensure that everybody is in the loop, on the career track, and part of the team. Making training available to everyone heads off claims of discrimination. And it is the right thing to do.

Although the numbers of people who fail to take training for any specific reason may be small, these numbers can add up. And so too can the effect on bottom-line productivity. Take a look at that effect in an imaginary but typical company.

All4One, LLC, is concerned that some groups do not take full advantage of its training offerings. Table 6-1 shows the results of a study they conducted.

All4One identified underrepresented groups and what percentage of the workforce in each group failed to take training. Only the primary reason for not taking training was considered, so there are not duplicates. All4One was shocked to realize that more than 40 percent of its employees either could not or would not take the training it offered.

All4One believes that e-learning may help. More than half of these non-trainees indicated they would take e-learning if it were designed to overcome their reasons for not taking training. Thus the company expects to be able to train an additional 21 percent of the workforce.

Because fully trained workers are 20 percent more productive than untrained workers, All4One hopes to boost its overall productivity by 4 percent by using e-learning to train 21 percent more workers. Table 6-1 summarizes this analysis.

Table 6-1. Opportunity to make training available to more.

Those Who Do Not Take Training Because They:	Percentage of Workforce
Are too busy.	8%
Would have to travel.	8%
Travel as part of job.	3%
Have difficulties with language.	3%
Face cultural barriers.	2%
Are older than mainstream.	8%
Are younger than mainstream.	5%
Have physical disabilities.	4%
= Total not taking training now	41%
× % that would take e-learning	50%
= Additional learners	21%
× % training increases productivity	20%
= Productivity boost	4%

Don't trust these figures? Then download the spreadsheet from the book's Website (www.horton.com/using) and plug in your own numbers.

The rest of this chapter looks at groups that may not be getting the training they need and for whom e-learning may provide a solution.

BUSY WORKERS

In scores of organizations, workers are simply too busy to take training. These are the people whose schedules are plastered with required meetings, whose beepers and mobile phones are constantly interrupting those meetings to call them away to yet another crisis. They are the people with irregular schedules or those who work swing shifts. Or they are just the people perennially assigned to the do-or-die projects.

Never mind that the training might make them more efficient and hence not so busy. They simply refuse to sign up for training because they cannot schedule the block of time required for conventional training.

How E-Learning Can Help

Properly designed e-learning can fit effective training into the schedules of busy people. E-learning does not require time for travel, so all the time spent in e-learning is spent learning. And asynchronous e-learning does not require learners to meet a fixed schedule. Learners can start at any time, take as long as necessary, and go as fast as desired.

Using E-Learning to Train Busy People

In designing, buying, and deploying e-learning to meet the needs of busy people, keep the following suggestions in mind.

Keep Courses Short and Focused. Busy people do not have the time or patience to sit through a long course just to acquire a few nuggets of knowledge or a single isolated skill. They cannot waste time on lessons and modules that cover things they already know or have no use for. So, you should:

☐ Design or buy short courses that can fit between major crises. Aetna used 15-minute lessons to broaden the appeal of its e-learning (Kroll, 1999).

☐ Use courses that cover just the essentials. Keep the course focused on its objectives.

☐ Include self-assessments within each module to let learners diagnose what they need to know and what they already know and hence can skip.

Let Learners Learn at Their Own Pace. Lightspeed Larry needs a quick overview and Pricilla Precision needs complete mastery. How can you satisfy both?

☐ Make it easy for learners to find the specific items they want to learn. Include a rich navigational scheme including a menu, index, course map, and search facility.

☐ Clearly differentiate optional and required material.

☐ Break long presentations into shorter modules that can be spaced out at a pace set by the learner. Spacing out presentations can significantly increase learning (Dempster, 1988). This effect is called the spacing effect.

Let Learners Learn 24x7. Design your e-learning to accommodate the time learners have available to take it. For example:

☐ Design e-learning to work on computers workers have access to—in their own offices, in offices they borrow, at home, and in the business center at the hotel.

☐ Let learners download lessons and access them from portable computers as they move about during the day. See the section "Mobile Workers" for more suggestions.

☐ Do not require real-time online meetings. Or record them so those who cannot attend can play back the meeting later.

Accommodate Interruptions. In many work environments, the MTBI (mean time between interruptions) is shorter than the average length of an e-learning module. The MTBI is not getting longer, so you should

☐ use short, self-contained modules that learners can complete between interruptions

☐ let learners bookmark their current location in the course so they can find it again after the interruption

☐ include frequent summaries and recaps so learners can quickly resume after an interruption.

Motivate, Motivate, Motivate. E-learning must compete for a share of the worker's time, attention, and passion. To ensure e-learning gets its full share, try these strategies:

☐ Advertise learning objectives that have clear and immediate value to learners. Make obvious why taking e-learning is as important as the crisis du jour.

☐ Make learning fun. Use rich interactivity and interaction, not just text to be read from the screen.

DISTANT WORKERS

Distance can be a barrier for anyone who must travel to the site of training. The time and costs required for travel limit attendance by employees from foreign and regional offices, factories, and research centers. Distant customers face the same limitations.

As a result, distant workers often neglect their training needs. They often feel left out of the mainstream of corporate life. Many feel that they are second-class employees. They may, in fact, not be on the career track because they lack training and because they lack informal contacts within headquarters. The organization as a whole suffers because course attendance is not representative of the diversity of the workforce.

Can E-Learning Reach Distant Learners?

E-learning's reach is global. Many organizations are using e-learning to train their most distant learners:

- Toys 'R' Us used Microsoft NetMeeting to train employees in 19 regional distribution centers how to operate new computer programs (Microsoft Corporation, 1998b). The training was enthusiastically received by employees who liked the flexibility this method provided and the access to remote experts.
- Using e-learning technologies, master trainers at ProSoft can in one day train 50 trainers throughout the United States on complex software packages (Ainslie, 1998).
- Rensselaer Polytechnic Institute in Troy, New York, conducted live training of learners 11 time zones away in Hong Kong (O'Keefe, 1997).
- Office Depot, Inc., used a virtual classroom to simultaneously train learners in Florida, California, and Texas, thus increasing enrollment by a factor of three while increasing learner satisfaction by 20 percent (Ellis, 1997).
- Lucent Technologies' Wireless University makes its e-learning courses available in 90 countries (Docent, 1999).

How E-Learning Can Help

E-learning can help integrate distant learners into mainstream corporate life. It can deliver consistent training at all locations. Collaboration within e-learning courses helps learners build contacts within the organization and within the industry. Employees in the headquarters office get exposure to the ideas and viewpoints of those working in the provinces.

Economics of Training Distant Workers

The Global Gastritis Foundation (GGF) provides free training to its employees, but the employee's department must still pay for their travel expenses and time while in training. Is free training really free? Table 6-2 shows their analysis of what a three-day "free" training costs departments depending on whether no travel is required, domestic travel (within the United States) is required, or international travel is required.

The first group of costs involves the employee's time for the days the employee is off the job. Domestic travel adds two days to the time of the class, and international travel adds four days (international flights are longer, and travelers have to recover from jet lag).

Daily expenses include the costs of hotel, food, rental car, and so forth. No such expenses are incurred when travel is not required. For domestic travel, the daily expenses ($200) must be paid for one day more than the length of the class. For international travel, it is two days more than the length of the class.

One last cost is that for airfare. For domestic travel, the average airfare is $800; for international travel, it is $1,800.

The free training is not really free. For those who must travel internationally, it is seven times less free than for those who do not have to travel. Table 6-2 summarizes this analysis.

Table 6-2. Costs for training distant workers.

Costs	No Travel	Domestic Travel	International Travel	
Days off job	3	5	7	days
× Employee time rate	$200	$200	$200	per day
= Cost of employee time	$600	$1,000	$1,400	
Days away from home	0	4	5	days
× Cost of hotel, food, rental car	$200	$200	$200	per day
= Daily expenses	$0	$800	$1,000	
+ Airfare	$0	$800	$1,800	
= Total cost to employee's dept.	$600	$2,600	$4,200	

If you want to compare the costs for your organization, download the spreadsheet from this book's Website (www.horton.com/using).

Using E-Learning to Train Distant Learners

To use e-learning to train distant learners, consider their needs and the constraints imposed by distance.

☐ Focus first on the courses that distant learners need and will take. Survey them to find their immediate needs. They may be avoiding your training because you lack the courses they need, not because travel is required.

- ☐ Involve distant employees in course development and setting standards. Not only will you improve your e-learning designs, you will also make valuable allies in distant places.

- ☐ Design for the kinds of computers and networks that are available in distant offices. Consider screen size, network speed, browser versions, plug-ins, and so forth. This book's companion Website (www.horton .com/using) links to forms to help in specifying technology.

- ☐ Do not depend on synchronous events. Problems with international synchronous courses include religious, business, and national holidays; time-zone shifts; and the unwillingness to participate during non-office hours.

- ☐ Use collaborative activities to help distant learners meet and befriend workers throughout the rest of the organization.

- ☐ Consider vacation schedules. For example, six-week vacations are common in Europe, and many people take vacations in August.

- ☐ Comply with foreign standards, regulations, and laws. Some nations have standards for IT ergonomics, privacy, and other aspects of computer usage. Germany, for example, forbids tracking employee actions without their permission. Also consider labor laws. In Scandinavia it is common for office workers to belong to a union, which may have a say in training issues.

- ☐ Accommodate cultural differences and language difficulties. (These are covered in other sections in this chapter.)

MOBILE WORKERS

Many workers are constantly on the road or in the air. Their office is Seat 24C on United Flight 807, and they rack up more miles in rental cars than their personal car. Those who travel are seldom at the right place and time to take conventional training. And they are not in the mood for more travel in order to take training.

How E-Learning Can Help

E-learning can make training available to those who, because of their frequent need to travel as part of their jobs, cannot be at the fixed location and time when conventional training is conducted. Furthermore, e-learning that can be taken while on the road gives business travelers a productive alternative to hanging out at the hotel bar at the end of the day.

Economics of Training Mobile Workers

RoadToad, Inc., is concerned with the cost of equipping its mobile salesforce to take e-learning, so they do a back-of-the-envelope calculation to calm their nerves. Table 6-3 shows their figures. They estimate that the necessary com-

Computers for Mobile Workers

The following list specifies a laptop computer specially configured for taking e-learning. This setup should be adequate for the next few years.

Component	Specification	Notes
Processor	Pentium III at 1 gigahertz	So multimedia will play smoothly and rapidly.
Memory	256 megabytes	So multimedia has lots of room to load, and the learner can run multiple programs at once.
Display size	1024 x 768 pixels	So complex graphics and intricate page layouts can be displayed.
Display colors	Millions (32-bit)	So high-fidelity color is possible.
Hard disk	30 gigabytes	So lessons can be stored locally when off the network.
CD-ROM (and DVD) drive	8X speed combination drive	For media too large to transmit over the network. (And for watching movies after completing lessons.)
Networking	10/100BaseTX Ethernet	So learners can hook up to high-speed networks when available.
Modem	56 K V.90	For times when high-speed networks are not available.
Wireless phone interface	(Depends on mobile phone)	As a last resort for connecting.
Sound	16-bit stereo output and input	For listening to voice narration and recording for voice-conferencing.
Headphones	Stereo	For listening to sounds and narration without disturbing the person in the next seat.
Spare batteries	Lithium ion	So the learning can go on and on and on.
External microphone	(Or combination head-phone-microphone)	For audioconferencing or recording voice messages or annotations.
Video camera	Color, 640 x 480 pixels, USB interface	For videoconferencing. (And to show how happy you are you found an Internet connection fast enough to handle video.)

As of November 2001, you could purchase a system like this for about $4,000.

puters will cost $4,000. These computers should last for three years (36 months) for a monthly cost of $111 for the computer. Additional costs would include an Internet Service Provider account for about $25 per month. Because employees will take about four courses a year, RoadToad budgets $60 per month for phone charges to cover taking one-third of the course. The total monthly charges are thus $196 a month. Since employees will take a course over an average of three months, the total costs are three times this, or a total of $588, in the same range as travel costs to take a classroom course. Table 6-3 summarizes this analysis.

Table 6-3. Costs of mobile learners.

Laptop computer	$4,000	
÷ Useful life	36	months
= Amortized cost	$111	per month
ISP account	$25	per month
Phone charges	$60	per month
Total monthly costs	$196	per month
× Time to complete course	3	months
= Per course costs	$588	per course

Why not download the spreadsheet from this book's Website (www.horton .com/using)? Consider some variants to these figures. If workers use the laptop for purposes other than e-learning, reduce that cost accordingly. What if phone charges are higher, or it takes less time to complete courses?

Using E-Learning for Mobile Workers

> **Model for Training Mobile Learners**
>
> ESTRELLA (www.estrella.org), a project funded by the U.S. Department of Education's Office of Migrant Education, provides the children of migrant workers with laptop computers and access to school programs that allow them to accumulate credit even as they move through several states over a single school year (Web-Based Education Commission, 2000).

To be of use to travelers, e-learning must overcome obstacles posed by its peripatetic participants. Travelers are not on the company intranet or the Internet continuously. Many destinations lack fast, reliable Internet connections. Learners may be stressed, tired, distracted, and lonely.

Here are some suggestions for the way to design and deploy e-learning to support these workers.

Design for Slow (or No) Network Connections. Make sure learning continues at full speed even when learners lack high-speed Internet connections.

☐ Design courses for low bandwidth connections. At least include low-bandwidth summaries.

☐ Design alternative versions that provide video, sound, and other large media elements on CD-ROM.

☐ Let learners download and go. Design courses so learners can download lessons to their hard disk and access them while not connected to the network. Some learning management systems can store tracking information locally and upload it when the learner reconnects to the network.

☐ Beware of courses that are multimedia extravaganzas or text read from the screen. Rich interactivity is preferred over rich media.

Let Learners Proceed at Their Own Pace. Make sure learners can take training at the time and place they choose.

☐ Do not require learners to meet a rigid time schedule. Make synchronous events truly optional. Let learners play them back later. Nothing on exams should depend on information communicated only during a synchronous event.

☐ Use a discussion forum to provide access to a community of fellow learners. Such a community can answer questions, solve problems, and emotionally support one another.

Design for Lonely, Tired Learners. Sally Salesrep just got back to her hotel room after an exhausting, frustrating day. She misses her family and her feet ache. How are you going to get her to take e-learning when she'd rather take a long hot bath or watch an in-room movie?

☐ Display objectives that make clear the value of taking the course to the individual learner, not just to the learner's organization. Travelers may consider travel time their own personal time and spend it grudgingly.

☐ Make learning fun. Use learning games and meaningful interactivity, especially activities involving online discussions with fellow learners.

☐ Keep visual designs, activities, and presentations simple. Do not require too much short-term memory or attention.

Make Accessing E-Learning Easier. It is not always easy for mobile learners to log onto e-learning. Take steps to remove obstacles:

☐ Book hotels with high-speed Internet access.

☐ Publish clear instructions on how to access training from the road. Include instructions on setting up the computer, phone numbers for Internet Service Providers, and log-on procedures.

☐ Provide plenty of dial-up ports. Or, contract with an Internet Service Provider who does.

☐ Create a single access procedure for e-learning and other corporate systems so traveling workers only have to log in once to take e-learning, get email, download and play voice messages (bandwidth permitting), check orders, and so forth.

☐ Provide toll-free numbers or telephone credit cards so learners don't pay hotel long-distance charges.

E-Learning on Handheld Wireless Devices?

The latest handheld wireless devices would seem ideal for delivering e-learning to traveling workers. After all, such devices are being used to enter and track orders, send and receive email, and look up reference information. Two e-learning systems, Generation 21(www.generation21.com) and Latitude 360 (www.latitude360.com) include the capability to deliver to mobile devices. But few extensive e-learning applications exist for wireless devices yet. The main limitations today are the relatively slow bandwidth of wireless connections, limited on-board memory of such devices, and the small screen size of units such a the Palm Pilot and Pocket PC. Next-generation devices and telecommunications standards should overcome these limitations. Until then, you can make a start by:

☐ using wireless training primarily for low-level cognitive skills and straightforward knowledge
☐ linking to existing information resources that are primarily text, so mobile workers can efficiently find information they need
☐ performing collaboration using textual media, such as discussion forums, chat, and instant messaging
☐ employing that portable medium called paper for complex information that requires showing large amounts of detail at once.

LEARNERS WITH LANGUAGE DIFFICULTIES

Language difficulties can prevent people from signing up for training and can make their learning experiences frustrating and embarrassing. Such difficulties face those who have English as a second language, those with dyslexia and other reading difficulties, and those with low verbal skills. These problems often go unreported because those who suffer them are embarrassed to admit the problem or feel it is their personal failing.

If you think those in your organization have perfect language skills, ponder these statistics. In the United States, 47 percent of the adult education courses taken were for English as a Second Language (http://www.cal.org /ncle/FAQS.HTM). According to the Office of Technology Assessment (OAT), a research organization of the U.S. Congress, 35 million adult Americans have trouble with literacy tasks. A Statistics Canada report put the rate of functional illiteracy at about 46 to 48 percent (www.geocities.com/Athens/Aegean /9318/literacy.html). Dyslexia afflicts 10 to 15 percent of Americans (www.dyslexia-add.org/).

It is no surprise that those with language difficulties shun the classroom where participants must listen to a rapidly speaking instructor, read slides flashed on the screen for just a few seconds, decipher handwritten notes, answer questions when called on, and debate fellow learners.

Many have trouble understanding words mumbled, spoken rapidly, or spoken with an unfamiliar accent. They also have trouble understanding slang and colloquialisms. They likewise have trouble reading text hand written on a board or overhead. They cannot write down notes quickly enough. Many feel self-conscious about their verbal skills and hence may not speak out in class or participate fully.

How E-Learning Can Help

Properly designed e-learning lets people process language at their own speed and get the assistance they need. In e-learning most of the core information is in text, not just in spoken words. Multimedia can be used to present the same information in text, spoken words, and in pictures. Learners can replay voice narration or multimedia segments including voice. In asynchronous discussions, they can take time to compose replies. At any time they can access online dictionaries, grammar guides, and technical glossaries.

Using E-Learning to Overcome Language Difficulties

E-learning can make understanding the language of a course easier and less stressful. Here are a few tips:

- ☐ Spell out expectations. Specify assumptions and requirements, especially concerning language skills, participation, and scoring criteria for tests and assignments that require use of language.
- ☐ Provide online training to help learners improve their language skills.
- ☐ Train designers, instructors, facilitators, and discussion moderators in how to overcome language difficulties.
- ☐ Provide a text transcript of all narration.
- ☐ Link e-learning to an online glossary, dictionary, and other language aids. Help learners find online translation dictionaries and translation services.
- ☐ Do not require participation in chat, instant messaging, or videoconferencing. Let learners respond asynchronously.
- ☐ Illustrate text with simple graphics and animation.
- ☐ Write in a simple, international style (see sidebar).

☐ Pick a narrator whose voice is especially clear, even after compression and when played through cheap computer speakers in a noisy room. Slow the pace to about 185 words per minute. Use Standard American English—no dialect or colloquialisms.

☐ Eliminate background noise, sound effects, and music while narration is playing. Let listeners concentrate on the voice.

Writing in an International Style

In e-learning, much of what you communicate will be in the form of spoken words or displayed text. Make those words understandable by as many as possible.

☐ Write in simple sentences. Use simple words and phrases.
☐ Avoid slang. Never say, "For a totally tubular learning experience surf on over to our gnarly education site, dude."
☐ Take care with pronunciation-dependent words, such as *conduct, progress, record, extract,* and *invalid.*
☐ Use few abbreviations and define them in the glossary. Use an abbreviation only if the term is used repeatedly, the term is more than three words long, or the abbreviation is better known than the full term.
☐ Use complete labels for critical buttons and links.
☐ Follow rules for correct usage. Stick with standard forms. Proofread carefully.

LEARNERS OF DIFFERENT CULTURES

The need for training across cultural boundaries has never been greater. Look around the classroom today. You see recent immigrants, guest workers, resident aliens, workers from foreign offices, and the natural cultural diversity of your home region. Selling courses over the Web means your audience could be anyone of any culture. International trade, global organizations, and seamless telecommunications are turning the global village into the global classroom.

Training people of widely different cultural values, traditions, and taboos can be exciting, enlightening, and an education in itself. Don't become so engrossed in celebrating diversity that you overlook the dangers and difficulties of trying to cost-effectively train people with a wide range of sometimes contradictory values and deeply set behaviors. Training programs designed for a narrow range of cultures often face difficulties or outright rejection when extended to those of different cultures (Lim, 1999).

How Culture Affects Training

Culture affects how people relate to one another, and that affects how they best communicate and learn. Here are a few of the aspects of culture that you need to account for in designing and deploying training.

Interpersonal Relationships. The ways people relate to others varies across cultures. Especially important in relationships is the role of status. Politeness and respect for authority and age are large factors in how people greet one another and work together. In some cultures, a junior member of a firm would never publicly disagree or even differ with the opinions of a senior. Also important is the fear of disgrace or looking foolish. In some training classes, it is forbidden to ask questions of senior managers because they could give an incorrect answer that would weaken their authority. In some cultures, instructors do not answer questions for the same reason. Likewise, assertiveness and risk taking are not universally accepted values. Nor is the desire for friendship and camaraderie.

Social Interaction. Relationships between individuals and groups can vary widely. American school children are encouraged to speak out in class and acknowledged for doing better than average. In one school in the Southwest, however, Navajo children complained when their pictures were posted in the hallway in recognition of their high grades (Bransford, Brown & Cocking, 1999). They felt embarrassed at being set apart from their peers. The role of cooperation and competition must be considered in all team and class activities. One organization found that they could use competitive games successfully in e-learning—except for their sales representatives who were already too competitive.

Pedagogical Traditions. Learning is somewhat habitual. People get used to learning in a particular way and that becomes their mental model for learning in general. In designing any training you should ask, "How are the learners used to learning?" What do they see as the role of the instructor: master who controls every aspect of the classroom, sage who dispenses wisdom, consultant available to ask questions, or friend to offer comfort and encouragement? What is the role of learners? Do they passively listen to the instructor; or do they actively question the instructor, debate other learners, and conduct independent inquiries? What is the role of questions? For the instructor to test (and perhaps humble) learners? Or, for learners to verify and expand their own knowledge?

A big issue in pedagogical traditions is what outcome learners are working for. Are they working to gain skills and knowledge that will benefit them in their career? Or are they just working to achieve a high grade or win a certificate required for employment or promotion? And what are the ethics of cheating? In some countries, it is said that cheating is acceptable and a way of demonstrating that learners are smarter than the teacher and hence worthy of promotion.

Symbology. Cultures vary in the symbolic meaning of many common emblems, colors, numbers, and so forth (Horton, 1994). For example, the use of the check mark to flag correct answers and the *X* for incorrect answers is common—but the use of these marks is opposite in Scandinavia. The color green may be associated with money in the United States, but not elsewhere where paper currency comes in a variety of colors.

Gender Issues. Views on acceptable gender roles vary around the globe and from culture to culture. Who speaks first in a conversation? Who has the last word? Who can interrupt someone else? What forms of emotion can be expressed? These are all issues of disagreement that can hinder productive discussion in training—as can issues of whether mixed gender teams are acceptable.

Modesty and Clothing. Cultures dress differently. Some show up for training in formal business attire and others in shorts, t-shirt, and sandals. Some wear traditional attire that covers the head and most of the body. Differences in clothing combined with inaccurate stereotypes can miscue relationships. Someone may assume that a Malaysian woman who covers her head in a scarf is reticent and retiring or that a Brazilian man in a business suit will be stuffy and formal. Differences in clothing can also make some participants self-conscious.

Religious Issues. People do not check their religious values at the classroom door. If you were conducting training in the Middle East, you would not invite participants to an after-class pig roast. But would you remember to schedule prayer breaks for Islamic participants?

How E-Learning Can Help

E-learning can make training more flexible and can diminish irrelevant differences that can lead to conflict.

E-learning is a new institution without so many expectations built in. There is more flexibility to define the rules of social interaction, based on the informality of the Web. It's a new world.

The lack of face-to-face contact that is often cited as a disadvantage for e-learning can actually make it more effective in multicultural training. Computer-mediated communications are more neutral and flexible. Anonymity and invisibility can let learners choose what aspects of their appearance and culture they choose to reveal. Fewer cultural issues arise and fewer negative stereotypes are triggered.

By designing a flexible e-learning program, you let people learn using a style that fits their culture and expectations. You can publish multiple versions of a course from a single source. Or let learners customize it on the fly.

Collaboration in e-learning provides learners opportunities to meet and interact with those of other cultures. E-learning can promote tolerance and understanding.

Using E-Learning for Those of Different Cultures

Teaching people of many different cultures is challenging. Here are a few tips to guide you in using e-learning for diverse groups of learners:

- ☐ Involve people from target cultures in your e-learning program. Include them in setting objectives, writing standards, and designing e-learning products. Don't rely on outdated stereotypes about what "they" want. Teach designers about the cultures they are designing for. And have your courses and modules reviewed by those who will be taking them.

- ☐ Take a middle road between cultural extremes: not too formal or too casual, not too authoritarian nor too free form. Mix different styles of learning activities: team work and individual work, drill-and-practice and discovery learning.

- ☐ Keep the design plain and simple. Favor neutral colors and earth tones. Limit flashing and blinking. Study the Websites of several successful international companies and emulate their businesslike style.

- ☐ Accommodate different pedagogical styles. Suggest a default path through the material, even if you do not require it. Build in navigation buttons that allow learners to take courses in a structured or unstructured fashion.

- ☐ Illustrate points with a variety of examples from different cultures.

- ☐ Define the rules of the e-learning culture. In particular, publish guidelines for interpersonal communications. Spell out the role of the instructor and the role of the learner. Allow learners to share as much or as little of their cultural identity as they choose.

- ☐ Help local-area experts adapt your e-learning products for their local culture. Make it easy for them to add and substitute material. Incorporate some of their best work in your original version.

- ☐ Avoid common symbolic misunderstandings. Avoid photographs and realistic drawings of people. Instead use cartoon characters of no specific gender, economic class, or age. Likewise avoid using animals, hand gestures, and human figures as symbols. If you use colors symbolically, define your meanings clearly.

- ☐ Do not pretend to be universal or completely neutral. If your course is based on how things are done in the United Kingdom, say so. Do, however, avoid overtly patriotic references and symbols, such as flags, national anthems, and military heroes. It is better to be a polite foreigner than a phony native.

OLDER LEARNERS

Older learners, for a variety of reasons, may face difficulties obtaining the training they need to stay current in their jobs and to prepare for new assignments.

Many older learners may have problems with hearing, eyesight, and mobility, Although disabilities affect only 19 percent of those in the age range 25 to 64, more than half of those 65 and older have disabilities, and 37 percent of them suffer from severe disabilities (McNeil, 2001). (Using e-learning for those with disabilities is covered elsewhere in this chapter.) Some older workers, who began their careers before computers and networks permeated all work activities, may lack advanced computer skills. But worse than any actual disabilities or lack of skills are the stereotypes about older workers: that they are senile, stubborn, forgetful, and set in their ways.

How E-Learning Can Help

E-learning can make training more accessible to older workers by overcoming limitations they face and by leveraging their strengths.

In well-designed e-learning, participants can repeat and retry segments as needed to compensate for anxiety and reduced short-term memory. Anonymity allows learners to fit more easily into a multi-age environment. Online you are any age you want to be.

E-learning provides a gentle and productive way for older learners to become proficient in new information technology skills without embarrassment—to collaborate and compete with younger workers.

E-learning removes the requirements to travel. Travel may be difficult because of health constraints or the need to stay near ailing spouses or parents.

Collaborative e-learning taps the wealth of experience and knowledge possessed by older workers. In the 1990s, many companies that "encouraged" their older workers to take early retirement had to hire these retirees back as consultants.

Challenges for Training Older Learners

To provide these benefits, e-learning must overcome some challenges. The format and procedures of e-learning may contradict lifelong experiences with learning. One worker nearing retirement asked: "Why should I learn a new way to learn? I've only got another nine months with the company?" Furthermore, many older workers may have negative stereotypes of e-learning stemming from bad experiences with "teaching machines" and computer-aided instruction of the past few decades.

Using E-Learning to Train Older Learners

Making e-learning work for older learners is not hard, provided you attend to their specific needs, values, and preferences. Here are a few tips:

☐ Provide training in the use of new information technologies that older workers may not be familiar with.

☐ Minimize reliance on recent or advanced technologies such as instant messaging and videoconferencing until learners have been trained in their use.

☐ Keep the design predictable, simple, consistent, and well organized. Limit trendy design elements, gratuitous graphics, and meaningless multimedia. Your e-learning should not look and sound like a music video. Aim for an attractive but businesslike look and feel.

☐ Proofread. Older workers went to school when grammar, punctuation, and spelling mattered. They may be annoyed and distracted by a casual approach to language.

☐ Take a respectful tone, not too cute or fresh, and never sarcastic. Older workers expect a certain amount of respect for their knowledge and experience.

☐ Establish telementoring relationships between younger and older workers. For example, G.E. Chairman Jack Welch (an "older worker" himself) required his senior executives to find mentors among younger workers with more Internet experience.

YOUNGER LEARNERS

Younger workers represent a special challenge for training. For one thing, they represent the future of the organization. They bring new ideas, energy, and risk-taking attitudes. They are generally self-reliant and independent. Unless they receive effective training, however, they are unlikely to mature into highly productive workers.

Studies of young workers and college students show that they have different training needs and preferences than their predecessors (Ruch, 2000).

Their tastes in media may be more sophisticated. They have logged more hours watching television than in school. Though skilled at extracting information from video and other dynamic media, they may have correspondingly lower verbal skills. Some, habituated to the fast pace of computer-mediated communications, may regard face-to-face meetings a waste of time.

Young workers are comfortable around computers and telecommunications devices (Frand, 2000). They use chat and instant messaging like older generations use the telephone. But be careful; their computer skills may be spotty—they may know how to download free music but lack knowledge of business applications.

Young workers are more interested in personal skills development than company loyalty. Few expect to stay with the same company throughout their career and hence are interested in developing portable skills they can take to the next job. They are impatient with training that doesn't meet their needs.

How E-Learning Can Help

E-learning provides younger learners a way to learn what they want to learn in a way that they find natural and fitting. E-learning occurs in a learning environment with which younger learners have positive associations—chatting with friends, downloading music, and so forth. It provides a way to leverage their computer skills in a way that demonstrates their value to their employers.

Self-directed e-learning fits the self-directedness and independence of young learners. It offers career development skills that they can use in whatever job they take on.

Using E-Learning to Train Younger Workers

Younger workers would seem a natural for e-learning. They are comfortable with technology, and they are independent thinkers. Here are a few suggestions to make the match even better:

- ☐ Spell out the advantages of training. Make clear how training helps younger workers do their immediate jobs and acquire skills they can take to future jobs.
- ☐ Let learners custom-tailor the e-learning to their needs. Include a rich navigation scheme (menu, map, index, search facility) so that they can find the parts of training they need at the moment.
- ☐ Use rich interactivity, such as learning games and simulations, so they can put their game-playing skills to work (Prensky, 1998).
- ☐ Use chat, instant messaging, and discussion forums freely. Remember, 90 million young people go into AOL chat rooms each day.
- ☐ If you use video, make it of the highest quality because younger learners have good video-watching skills.
- ☐ Don't expect young learners to read long passages of text. Use more interactivity, animation, and video.
- ☐ Add plenty of self-assessments in each module to lock in learning immediately. This is a good practice for learners brought up on television and sound bites.
- ☐ Establish telementoring relationship with older learners. Each can learn from the other. Older, more senior workers can teach how things work "in here" and younger workers, how things work "out there."

LEARNERS WITH DISABILITIES

Training departments worldwide are scrambling to make training available to those with common physical disabilities. Doing so expands the talent pool their companies can draw from. And it helps them comply with legal requirements such as the Americans with Disabilities Act, the Telecommunications Act, and Section 508 of the Rehabilitation Act.

Disabilities and E-Learning

Making training accessible to those with disabilities is expensive. The costs of retrofitting training centers with ramps and elevators, especially ones in old buildings, are quite high. As are the costs of hiring signers to interpret for the deaf. Many see e-learning as a more economical and effective way to overcome disabilities.

Numbers of People with Disabilities. The Americans with Disabilities Act of 1990 defines a disability as a limitation in a major life activity. In 1997, by that definition, 19 percent of the U.S. population between 25 and 64 years of age was disabled, and 12 percent had a severe disability (McNeil, 2001). Twelve percent have employment difficulties because of disabilities.

These statistics understate the problem because people sometimes acquire situational disabilities. Although not confined to a wheelchair, trainers frequently drag around a dolly of computers and handouts and confront the same lack of ramps and elevators that bar entrance to those who are. When people connect over a slow modem, they often turn off the display of graphics, rendering them blind to the information communicated only in those graphics. When someone closes their eyes to cope with a migraine headache, they are temporarily blind. Designing for those with disabilities helps everyone.

How E-Learning Can Help. E-learning can help by using Internet technologies to surmount the obstacles faced by those with physical disabilities. E-learning removes one set of barriers. It travels to learners, not the other way around. Travel can be difficult for those who cannot see or hear or walk unassisted. Travel also requires those with disabilities to leave their homes and offices where they have technologies and other aids to help with their disabilities.

E-learning can also help by presenting information in multiple media and forms. Those who cannot hear can read text transcripts, and those who cannot see can hear text read aloud.

Collaborative e-learning lets learners choose whether and when to reveal disabilities. Often the biggest disability is in the minds of fellow learners.

Challenges for E-Learning. Making e-learning accessible for everyone will pose a challenge for e-learning. For one thing, only 40 percent of those with a disability have used computers, in contrast with 75 percent rate for those without a disability (Falling Through the Net: Toward Digital Inclusion, 2000).

Making e-learning accessible adds to the development and testing process. Some of these costs may be mandated by the need in the United States to comply with Section 508 of the Rehabilitation Act, which requires federally funded facilities to make their information technology applications equally accessible to those with disabilities as to those without.

Not only must you manage the costs of compliance but the complexity as well. Redundancy among various media can add clutter and contradictions among solutions. What's needed for the deaf may raise barriers for the blind or mobility impaired. None of these problems should dissuade you, but you should be realistic in budgets and schedules.

General Solutions

Begin with strategies and general solutions that will help with all or multiple disabilities. Later sections of this chapter offer suggestions on designing for specific disabilities.

Don't Try to Solve the Whole Problem Alone. Within the training and information technology industries, other smart people are working to make technology accessible. Within your own organization, there are probably other groups working on this same issue. If you are responsible for training internal employees, work with the human resources and information technology departments for a common strategy on opening job positions to those with disabilities. If your training supports your company's products, find out what strategies are being used by the product development team to make the product's user interface accessible. Monitor what accessibility aids are built into browsers and operating systems. Build on the work of others.

Learn About Disabilities. Educate your designers, instructors, facilitators, discussion moderators, and others involved in e-learning on how to work with and design for those with disabilities. Learn about legal requirements, about accessibility aids in operating systems, about third-party accessibility add-ons, about accessible browsers, and about Websites and tools for testing the accessibility of your e-learning. (See the section "Resources for Making E-Learning Accessible" later in this chapter.) Locate good advice beyond that offered here.

Provide Alternatives for Basic Operations. Provide more than one way to get required information and to perform required tasks. Let learners input words by speaking or typing, absorb verbal material by listening or reading, and navigate by mouse or keyboard.

Provide Additional Ways of Learning. Rather than providing one course for everyone, consider finding or producing alternative learning products that learners can pick from. Blend forms or have alternatives, rather than trying to make every page accessible by everyone. For example, consider purchasing electronic books, which can be read aloud by screen readers.

Develop an Accessible Framework. Don't try to retrofit accessibility onto your courses. Develop a course shell with accessibility built in, and use this shell as the basis for courses you create. Likewise, develop accessible page templates and component templates. Create a library of scripts and objects for speech synthesis, speech recognition, and keyboard shortcuts. And teach course authors how to use these shells, templates, scripts, and objects.

Let Disabled Learners Participate as Equals. Double check to make sure your e-learning does not penalize those with disabilities. Eliminate timed tests or modules and allow plenty of time for response in real-time conferences. Or forgo real-time events altogether. Allow alternative formats for submitting work.

Target Specific Disabilities. Which disabilities are most common among your learners? For example, many baby boomers have nerve deafness and presbyopia. Color blindness is common in Scandinavia. For what subjects are there no accessible training products available? Prioritize and budget your efforts to target disabilities that most severely limit learning in your organization.

Follow the advice in the immediately following sections. They contain practical tips in using and designing e-learning to overcome specific disabilities. Do these things while you are researching even more things to do and better ways to do them.

Resources for Making E-Learning Accessible

Here are some resources you may find helpful in making your e-learning (and other online materials) accessible to those with common disabilities.

World Wide Web Consortium Guidelines. The W3C provides guidance to developers of Web and Internet technologies. For issues of accessability, the W3C provides these guidelines:

- ☐ W3C Web Content Accessibility Guidelines (http://www.w3.org/TR /WAI-WEBCONTENT/) spells out how to make Web-based content accessible by those with disabilities.
- ☐ W3C Techniques for Web Content Accessibility Guidelines (www .w3.org/TR/WAI-WEBCONTENT-TECHS/) provides suggestions on how to comply with the Web Content Accessibility Guidelines.

Assistive Technology and Information on Accessibility. For help making your course or Website accessible, consider these resources:

- ☐ Trace Center (www.tracecenter.org/) at the University of Wisconsin-Madison consolidates information on designing for those with disabilities.
- ☐ Bobby (www.cast.org/bobby), a Web-based testing service, can evaluate the accessibility of your Web-based materials.

Assistance Meeting Legal Requirements. For help complying with U.S. federal requirements to make e-learning accessible, consult these resources:

- ☐ Americans with Disabilities Act Homepage (www.usdoj.gov/crt/ada /adahom1.htm) includes resources made available by the U.S. Department of Justice to assist in compliance with the ADA.
- ☐ The Access Board (www.access-board.gov) is a U.S. federal agency devoted to developing and enforcing accessibility standards for federal agencies and federally funded facilities.
- ☐ Electronic and Information Technology Accessibility Standards (www.access-board.gov/sec508/508standards.htm) details compliance issues for the 1998 amendments to Section 508 of the Rehabilitation Act.
- ☐ Telecommunications Act Accessibility Guidelines (www.access-board .gov/telecomm/html/telfinal.htm) spells out requirements for accessible information technology under the Telecommunications Act.

Accessibility Tools for Computer Operating Systems. Recent versions of computer operating systems can simplify making information accessible. For Windows and Macintosh systems, consult these sites:

- ☐ Microsoft Accessibility (www.microsoft.com/enable/) is a starting point for learning about accessibility tools and techniques for Microsoft operating systems and products.
- ☐ Apple Computer's People with Special Needs (www.apple.com /disability/) contains information on Apple's technologies for making information accessible to those with disabilities.

Mobility Impairments

Mobility impairments affect 8.4 percent of working-age Americans (McNeil, 2001). This number includes those who have difficulty walking (4.2 percent); those with difficulty navigating stairs (6.6 percent); those who use a wheelchair (0.6 percent); and those who require a cane, crutches, or walker (1.5 percent). Those with mobility impairments may find it difficult to travel to the site of conventional training.

To help people with such disabilities, simply make e-learning available on the computers they have in their offices and homes, thereby removing the requirement to travel. Survey this segment of your potential learners to learn what computers and network connections they have. Design accordingly, or make provisions to upgrade their computers.

Dexterity Limitations

Many people lack precise eye-hand coordination because of strokes or palsy. According to U.S. Bureau of the Census figures, 2.6 percent of Americans in their prime working years have difficulty grasping objects (McNeil, 2001). Such dexterity limitations make difficult common actions like writing, typing, or manipulating a mouse precisely and smoothly. To help overcome such limitations:

☐ Ensure that the accessibility aids built into the operating system provide keyboard equivalents for mouse movements.

☐ Build in keyboard shortcuts for operations in your course. Do not make the mouse the only way to do anything.

☐ Enable speech-recognition for chat and other typing tasks.

☐ Make buttons, hypertext links, and other targets for mouse clicks large enough.

☐ Put no time limits on tests, especially ones that require pointing, clicking, or typing.

Visual Impairments

Visual impairments include color blindness, limited vision, and complete blindness. Each imposes different requirements for e-learning.

Color Blindness. Color blindness is the inability to distinguish among colors. The most common form of color blindness is a decrease in the ability to distinguish between red and green. This form of color blindness affects 5 to 10 percent of men and about 0.5 percent of women. A rarer form of color blindness fails to distinguish between blue and yellow. Total color blindness, or achromatopsia, is an inability to distinguish any colors. It affects only about one person in 33,000. To overcome problems with color blindness, ensure adequate light-dark contrast in all graphics and other displays. Make sure all displays work in black and white and then add color to make them work better for those without color blindness.

Also, pick color combinations that are less prone to misinterpretation by those with color blindness. Especially avoid using red-green differences for critical distinctions (like *stop* vs. *go* in a traffic light).

Limited Vision. Those with limited vision may have difficulty seeing small details, reading low-contrast text, or noticing objects in peripheral vision. In the age range 25 to 64, 2.6 percent of Americans have difficulty reading words and letters in a newspaper or on a computer screen (McNeil, 2001). To reduce the problems they face when taking e-learning, do the following:

☐ Make important items prominent and large. Do not require that learners notice small details—no small buttons or other targets.

☐ Minimize use of small details that are not enlarged by changing the base text size in the browser's settings. Otherwise let learners click to see an enlargement.

- [ ] Ensure adequate foreground/background contrast in text. Avoid color-on-color blocks of text. Test by printing out the page in black and white.
- [ ] Test your pages with the screen magnifier included with the accessibility aids for your operating system. Also test by enlarging the base text size in your browser's settings.

Blindness. Blindness affects 0.5 percent of Americans in their prime working years (McNeil, 2001). To help blind learners access your e-learning, make it possible for them to get information that is displayed visually. One of the best ways is to make provisions for screen readers, which are tools that can read aloud the text displayed on the computer screen. To accommodate screen readers:

- [ ] Provide alternative text for graphics, applets, embedded objects, and image maps. Provide the information that is lost by not seeing the visual image.
- [ ] Provide an optional text description of animation and video clips and a transcript of all voice narration. Make sure learners can search for this text and that it is accessible to screen readers. Also make voice-over narration for video and animation complete in itself. And make it easy to replay.
- [ ] Use ALT (or NAME or LABEL) attributes to provide text for all graphics. Do not just say "Red diagonal bar" but "Click to exit." If the graphic contains words, put those words in the ALT tag too.
- [ ] Provide text menus for all items in image maps.
- [ ] Do not create graphic-only pages or use JavaScript to generate text.
- [ ] Simplify the layout of the screen. Minimize the use of framesets, layers, and complex table schemes. Use just a few layouts and keep them the same throughout.
- [ ] If the screen layout is complex, provide an alternative page (for example in a NOFRAMES tag) that is just text, arranged for easy reading by a screen reader. Make the page a text summary of the content.
- [ ] Label links clearly. Make clickable text complete enough to make destination predictable. Screen readers let learners tab through the page stopping on such links. If your link is labeled "Click here," what does the learner hear?
- [ ] Provide keyboard equivalents to all mouse actions. Remember to incorporate keyboard shortcuts in Flash animations, Java applets, and Active X controls.
- [ ] To test your pages, turn off graphics and disconnect the mouse.

Hearing Impaired

The hearing impaired include those with some hearing loss as well as those with no appreciable hearing (deaf).

Limited Hearing. Those who are hard of hearing cannot hear soft sounds or certain frequencies. According to the U.S. Bureau of the Census, 2.4 percent of Americans in their prime working years have difficulty understanding conversations. Such a loss of hearing is common among who have suffered prolonged exposure to loud sounds. To make e-learning easier for them:

- [ ] Make voices especially distinct. Omit background music or sound effects while voice narration is present.
- [ ] Provide earphones and perhaps an external amplifier. Make sure earphones work with hearing aids.
- [ ] Use high-quality audio and require at least fast-modem connection for sound.

Deafness. Those who are deaf cannot hear sounds at all. Deafness affects 0.2 percent of Americans in their prime working years (McNeil, 2001). Some can read lips and understand sign language. To make e-learning accessible to the deaf:

- [ ] Provide transcripts of all voice narration, or a text summary of all animations and other situations where voice narration was used.
- [ ] Allow learners to pause animations and video while they read narration. Make replaying segments easy too.
- [ ] If you use video talking heads, make them close-ups with lip movements clearly visible. Some, but not all, deaf learners can read lips.
- [ ] Do not require audio conferencing by learners. Deaf learners cannot understand and may be self-conscious about speaking. The same applies for videoconferencing unless all participants understand sign language and the video is clear and fast enough to make signing practical.

Speech Impairments

Speech impairments affect 0.8 percent of working-age Americans (McNeil, 2001). Learners with speech impairments may not be able to speak clearly, or they may not be able to speak at all. The problem is the difficulty others have understanding the speaker and resulting self-consciousness of the speaker. To overcome these limitations:

- [ ] Do not require learners to speak. Offer chat and discussion forums as alternative channels.
- [ ] Use text-to-speech synthesis to generate an understandable voice.
- [ ] Require computers with high-quality sound input and output. Better quality sound processing results in more understandable voices on the other end of the line.
- [ ] Enable practice. Allow learners to hear themselves as others do. Provide a way to record, transmit, receive, and play back voices. That way, learners can adjust their voices for best recognition. This works well for anyone who wants to be understood at the other end of the line.

◀◀ ◀◀ ◀◀ ◀◀ ◀◀ ▶▶ ▶▶ ▶▶ ▶▶ ▶▶

YOUR TURN

Consider how e-learning can make high-quality training available to everyone in your organization. For each of the groups identified in this chapter, estimate how many fail to receive the training they need and how many of these could be reached by well-designed e-learning. Then, on worksheet 6-1, list a few things you will do to bring e-learning to each group.

	Worksheet 6-1. Making training available to more people.		
Group	**Number Who Fail to Receive Adequate Training**	**Number Who Can Be Served by E-Learning**	**How to Use E-Learning to Reach This Group**
Busy workers			
Those at distant locations			
Workers who travel			
Those with language difficulties			
Those of different cultures			
Older learners			
Younger learners			
Those with disabilities			

7

Accomplishing General Learning Goals

If you were to look at the strategic objectives of training departments and educational institutions, you would find that some general objectives are especially common. From Neolithic times onward, those charged with the education and training of others have fretted over how to get novices started, how to turn novices into experts, how to enable people to learn on their own, and how to ensure that learning is applied in productive work. E-learning does not alter these objectives, but it does afford some new tools in accomplishing them.

GETTING BEGINNERS STARTED

Getting started in a field is often the hardest part of learning. Beginners do not know the basic vocabulary or concepts of the field. Beginners don't know what they need to know. Beginners don't know how much they already know. Beginners must often do a great deal of work before they see any significant progress. Beginners need a starting point and propulsion.

In the field of computer programming, the problem of getting learners started is sometimes called the "Hello World" phenomenon. When learning a new programming language, the hardest program to write is the one that learners traditionally write at the beginning. It just displays the words "Hello World." Though only a few lines long, it is said to be the only original computer program written; everything else is elaboration and refinement.

In getting beginners started, the goal is not a high level of proficiency but achieving a critical level of knowledge and skill that enables one to become an independent learner or just an efficient learner.

How E-Learning Can Help

For beginners, e-learning can offer a quicker start to training, more efficient learning, and a more encouraging learning experience.

E-learning can be more efficient if it teaches just what the individual learner needs to know. Well-designed e-learning lets learners start from different points. Considerable time and enthusiasm can be saved by letting each individual start at a different point. Not everybody is equally uninformed, and not everybody needs the same prerequisites. Frequent, private assessments let learners gauge their own level of knowledge and pick from menus to fill in the gaps. The private nature of e-learning reduces embarrassment at having to admit to these gaps. And asynchronous e-learning can begin the day the employee accepts a new job. The employee does not have to wait for a class to start.

Economics of Getting Beginners Started

How can getting beginners started benefit an organization economically? Figure 7-1 shows a model for the effects of training on productivity. Though quite simple, this model does illustrate the important effect learning has on overall productivity. The model shows the profile of an individual's productivity over time. It is not to scale, but it does illustrate the three main phases of productivity growth. During the first phase, from the time the person is hired to the time he or she receives initial training, the person is considered a beginner. During the middle phase, the person moves from novice to expert in his or her job. But, at some point, the person's productivity levels off, not because he or she stops learning but because his or her rate of learning is just sufficient to keep up with the new developments in their field.

The subject of turning novices into experts, discussed later in this chapter, will consider the effects of e-learning during the novice phase of this model. But for now, the focus is on using e-learning for initial training.

Figure 7-1. Profile of rising productivity and the effect of training.

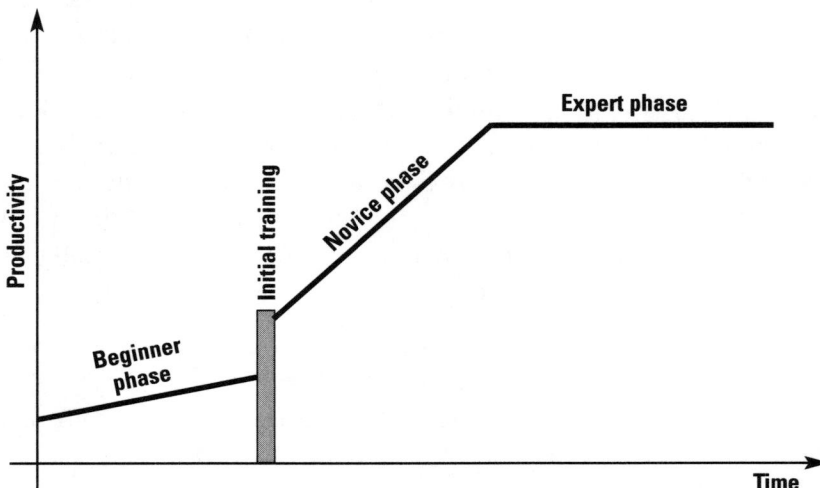

The Ground-Up Coffee Company is concerned with production. Giving employees unlimited samples of its own product has not helped. Now they are looking at e-learning to perk up production. Table 7-1 shows a comparison of two scenarios that differ only in the timing and results of initial training. Scenario A represents the current situation, and Scenario B the one using e-learning for initial training. The analysis covers productivity for a person who holds a job for 500 days. Productivity and production are measured in arbitrary units, which might represent beans roasted, cans filled, or sales completed.

Newly hired workers have an initial productivity of 10 units per day. This productivity rises gently as they observe and imitate their co-workers. The rate of increase is 0.2 units per day. In Scenario A, beginners must wait 30 work-days before receiving initial training, but in Scenario B they receive initial training after five days. The training in Scenario B is somewhat more effective, boosting productivity to 30 units per day, five units a day more than the training in Scenario A. In both cases initial training takes two days. This means that production during the beginner phase was 390 units in Scenario A but only 52.5 in Scenario B, not because the employee in Scenario B was less productive, but because the beginner phase was much shorter.

During the novice phase, the worker grows toward expert performance. The only differences here are that the worker in Scenario B starts at a higher level of productivity and hence the length of time required to reach expert level is shorter. The production is less for Scenario B, again because the time spent in this phase is shorter.

During the expert phase, productivity is the same. However, because the worker in Scenario B reached expert level first, the length of time at this level is longer and thus production is higher.

The totals show that Scenario B achieved higher overall production, 8 percent in fact, than Scenario A. It may seem ironic that the main payoff from improved initial training occurs during the expert phase of the worker's employment.

As always, the spreadsheet is available on the book's Website (www.horton .com/using). Download it and experiment if you wish. Why not try some different times during initial training and some different productivity rates after training?

Using E-Learning to Get Beginners Started

Getting learners started requires good research, a sound instructional design, and clever use of e-learning features.

Table 7-1. Effect of initial training on production.

	Scenario A	Scenario B	
Total time in job	500	500	days
Beginner Phase			
Initial productivity	10	10	units per day
Improvement as beginner	0.2	0.2	units per day
Time until initial training	30	5	days
Productivity after initial training	25	30	units per day
Length of initial training	2	2	days
Production as beginner	390	52.5	units per day
Novice Phase			
Productivity at start	25	30	units per day
Expert phase productivity	80	80	units per day
Improvement as novice	0.3	0.3	units per day
Time to expert phase	183	167	days
Production as novice	9,625	9,167	units
Expert Phase			
Expert phase productivity	80	80	units per day
Time as expert	285	326	days
Production as expert	22,773	26,107	units
Total			
Production	32,788	35,326	units
Improvement		2,538	units
		8%	

Set Clear, Tight Objectives. Specify precisely and unambiguously the goal of getting beginners started.

- ☐ Make sure everyone knows that the objective of training is to get beginners started, not to teach all about a subject and not to achieve high levels of expertise.
- ☐ If the subject is generic, shop around for an existing course. Many others have the same need. If no course is available, consider marketing your course to others.
- ☐ Research your potential learners so you can provide training that starts exactly at their level of skill and ends with the desired minimal proficiency.

Assess Current Levels of Knowledge. Don't assume a specific prior level of subject matter knowledge. Assess current levels of knowledge. Design the course so learners of varying levels of prior knowledge can all get started smoothly. To do so, let learners skip what they already know. Use automatically scored, anonymous tests to let learners privately assess their own knowledge and decide whether to take the entire course or just specific modules. You could even structure the course as a knowledge-driven tutorial in which learners progress through a series of assessments until they reach their level of prerequisite knowledge—at which point, they jump into the main flow of the course.

Guide Learners. When learners start in a new subject, they need higher levels of learning support than they do later (Carroll, 1990). Such "training wheels" can be removed as learners conquer early difficulties. In initial e-learning, however, use activities that guide learners as they gain exposure to a subject. Here are some examples:

- ☐ guided tours that lead learners through a Website, computer application, online document, or other electronic artifact
- ☐ step-by-step, hands-on activities that let learners "do it now and understand it later"
- ☐ guided analysis activities that step learners through examining a complex situation and noticing its pertinent details
- ☐ drill-and-practice for vocabulary and rote knowledge
- ☐ canned demonstrations so beginners can watch an expert perform procedures and demonstrate desired behaviors
- ☐ new material related to what learners already know and to real-world situations learners are familiar with.

Make Learning Fun. Make learning experiences positive and rewarding. Provide lots of concrete activities and opportunities for success.

- ☐ Promise anonymity. "No one will be watching you." Never embarrass learners.
- ☐ Use simple learning games, such as a crossword puzzles to teach vocabulary.
- ☐ Link to lots of real-world examples.

Structure Simply. Gently lead learners through the subject matter. Let them set the pace, but provide an efficient path through the material (even if only a default). Provide a "next" button to navigate this path.

Adopt a cookbook approach. Build up little ideas and skills, then integrate them into a whole. At each point let learners assess their understanding. Such an immediate opportunity to practice tells learners whether they understand the unit well enough to proceed to the next unit. Remember, beginners cannot self-evaluate.

Help Learners Navigate Confidently. Give the opening screen and homepage a welcoming, friendly look. Feature a light tone and even a whimsical design. Use soft edges, pastel colors, and engaging graphics. Keep the screen uncluttered. Remember that even experienced computer users can be overloaded by subject matter they do not understand.

Do not let learners get lost. Include a map of the course with a "You-are-here" indicator. Show interrelationships among concepts, procedures, and skills. Make clear how what the user is now learning relates to the whole.

Provide clear indicators of progress. Remind learners of what they have learned. If necessary, include arbitrary indicators (e.g., Module 8 of 12) or a graphical progress bar.

Build Scaffolding. When introducing a difficult concept, take special steps to ensure that the beginner is not overwhelmed, that is, build a scaffold. As the learner begins to master the concept, gradually expose the full complexity of the subject, that is, fade the supports. Some types of scaffolding and fading include those listed in table 7-2.

Table 7-2. Techniques of scaffolding and fading.

Scaffolding	Fading
Postpone difficult steps and start with the simpler and more interesting aspects of the subject. For example, in teaching use of a computer program, start with the program already installed and set up.	Require the learner to perform more difficult tasks.
Prompt for answers. Give the learner a form to fill in to structure their answers.	Ask open-ended questions with free-form answers.
Start with the simple, pure cases that fit the classical definitions and categories exactly.	Introduce borderline cases, exceptions, and gray areas. Link to Web searches that show a variety of answers.
Give explicit, detailed instructions of not only what to do but also how to do it.	Specify what to accomplish but not how.
Provide lots of detailed examples to emulate.	Specify general standards and guidelines.

Provide Assistance and Safety Nets. If beginners are new at e-learning as well as new to the subject matter, start with a synchronous, virtual classroom that mimics familiar classroom training—even if this means delaying the start of training to wait for a class to form. Or have learners take e-learning in a training center where computers are set up and maintained by the center staff and where assistance is available at any time. At least make sure that the neophyte e-learner can ask questions and get help at any time via instant messaging or plain old telephone.

Include ways for learners to ask questions about the subject. Set up a subject matter hotline. Make sure that learners know there is a human being to answer their questions. Include a subject matter FAQ file and a glossary with terms defined in words that beginners can understand.

TURNING NOVICES INTO EXPERTS

Experts differ from novices not just in the scope of their knowledge but in how they solve problems, reason, and learn. They also differ greatly in their job productivity. Therefore, there is great interest in turning novices into experts as rapidly as possible. The goal in training novices is to elevate the minimally proficient to full proficiency, increasing not just their knowledge but their problem-solving and reasoning skills as well.

How Experts Differ from Novices

Research has identified significant differences between experts and novices (Bransford, Brown & Cocking, 1999):

- Experts notice patterns and significant features that novices miss. Experts in fields as diverse as chess, mathematics, electronics, computer programming, physics, and radiology all showed sensitivity to meaningful patterns and configurations.
- Experts are better able to see the implications of the patterns and features they notice (deGroot, 1965).
- Experts have a large and well-organized body of subject matter knowledge (Chi, Feltovich & Glaser, 1981).
- Experts have knowledge organized around key concepts (Glaser & Chi, 1988).
- Experts can apply their knowledge in real-world contexts. Novices know isolated facts. Experts solve problems by first identifying useful concepts; novices immediately try to apply rote procedures and formulas (Chi, Feltovich & Glaser, 1981; Larkin, 1983).
- Experts can easily retrieve the knowledge they need in a given situation.

A lot of anecdotal evidence among managers and executives points up another difference: Experts are much more productive than novices. In some fields, such as computer programming and petroleum geology, the difference in productivity between novice and experts can be factor of 10 to 1 or even 100 to 1.

How E-Learning Can Help

E-learning, like any form of training, can help novices become experts more quickly and make their ultimate level of expertise higher. E-learning can do these things with less expense and disruption for the organization and the budding expert.

E-learning can provide efficient access to the breadth of training and depth of information required to become and stay an expert in a field. Well-designed e-learning provides deeper learning experiences than conventional training (McGrath, 1998). E-learning encourages learners to take longer to respond and think through their answers more deeply (Karayan & Crowe, 1997).

Web technology promotes collaborative and cooperative learning among novices and experts (McGrath, 1998). Learners who use Web technologies to discuss issues, research questions, and solve problems improve their critical reasoning, problem solving, and creativity (Baron & Goldman, 1994).

E-learning provides more experience in less time. Through open-ended simulations and drill-and-practice activities, it can provide unlimited opportunities to try out knowledge and skills and to learn by experience. Online assessments can provide continual feedback, so learners can monitor their current levels of expertise and focus that learning on filling gaps.

Economics of Turning Novices into Experts

The Ground-Up Coffee Company now wants to investigate the potential economic benefits of turning novices into experts. They use the same model of productivity introduced in the segment on getting beginners started. Table 7-3 shows the results of investing in building expertise. The first phase through initial training is the same in both scenarios, but in the "improvement as novice" phase, the assumption is that the rate of learning is higher (0.5 vs. 0.3), and that the ultimate level of productivity is higher (100 vs. 80). The result is a 26 percent improvement in productivity during the tenure of the worker in Scenario B.

This spreadsheet is available from the book's Website (www.horton .com/using). You way want to try some what-if experiments, such as varying the rate of improvement of a novice or combining improvements in initial training and novice training.

Using E-Learning to Turn Novices into Experts

Turning novices into experts is a complex process, not a single course. It requires using e-learning techniques and technologies to help novices acquire the characteristics of experts. Here are some tactics to try.

Table 7-3. Effect of building expertise on productivity.

	Scenario A	Scenario B	
Total time in job	500	500	days
Beginner Phase			
Initial productivity	10	10	units per day
Improvement as beginner	0.2	0.2	units per day
Time until initial training	5	5	days
Productivity after initial training	30	30	units per day
Length of initial training	2	2	days
Production as beginner	52.5	52.5	units per day
Novice Phase			
Productivity at start	30	30	units per day
Expert phase productivity	80	100	units per day
Improvement as novice	0.3	0.5	units per day
Time to expert phase	167	140	days
Production as novice	9,167	9,100	units
Expert Phase			
Expert phase productivity	80	100	units per day
Time as expert	326	353	days
Production as expert	26,107	35,300	units
Total			
Production	35,326	44,453	units
Improvement		9,127	units
		26%	

Teach What Experts Know. To develop expertise, explicitly teach learners to recognize important patterns of information (Bransford et al., 1989). Hyperlink to lots of real-world examples, case studies, analyses, and reports. Use multimedia to teach major principles and how to recognize them at work in real-world examples.

Help learners conditionalize knowledge, that is, learn where it applies (Glaser, 1992). In case studies, for example, focus on when to apply principles, techniques, and solutions. Annotate case studies via hyperlinks or annotations in PDF to point out concepts at work.

Teach Crucial Concepts and Patterns. Provide lots of practice, perhaps through simulation or drill-and-practice, aimed at teaching learners to recognize meaningful patterns. Chess players require 50,000 to 100,000 hours of practice to reach the level of world-class master. At that level they can recognize 50,000 patterns of pieces on the chessboard (Simon, 1973). Electronic activities can provide many opportunities for meaningful practice over a relatively short period of time.

Experts, because they attempt to understand problems before trying to solve them, may take longer to solve a problem than novices, who jump immediately to a solution strategy (Bransford, Brown & Cocking, 1999). Perhaps this means you should encourage novices to take the time to identify applicable concepts. Require learners to identify the principles, concepts, and patterns active in real-world examples. Tests can require them to provide the reasons for their conclusions, not just the answers.

Teach How to Find Reliable Sources. Experts may not know the answer ahead of time, but they almost always know how to find the answer quickly. To expand learners' ability to find answers, use scavenger hunt activities that require learners to search the Web and other information resources for reliable knowledge.

Provide Realistic Learning Experiences. Experts can solve problems amid the complexity of real life. Novices are traditionally limited to schoolbook problems abstracted down to the barest of details. You can help novices gain expertise by providing richer, more lifelike activities, such as these:

- ☐ examine-and-critique activities that require learners to examine real-world examples, case studies, and analyses and identify their strengths and weaknesses
- ☐ multiperspective activities that require learners to examine subjects from different viewpoints (can include role-playing activities and mock debates carried out in discussion forums)
- ☐ compound activities that, for example, require learners to perform research on a subject on the Web, interview experts via email, discuss opinions in a forum, vote on a proposal—all on the same subject.

Encourage Meta-learning. Experts are expert not just in their fields of endeavor but also in learning more about that field. This knowledge about how to learn effectively is called meta-learning and is especially important in helping experts maintain high levels of expertise. E-learning can help people monitor the level of their knowledge. Frequent and in-depth assessments can compare their capabilities with those of experts.

Connect Learners with Experts. One of the fastest ways to build expertise, especially in a rapidly advancing or ill-defined field, is to increase the contacts novices have with experts. Experts provide advice, insights, and role models. The trick is to engineer such contacts so they do not take experts away from their work for too long, and so that experts get as much from the exchanges as do novices. Here are some suggestions:

- ☐ Prepare learners to meet experts. Hyperlink to biographies and examples of the works of experts.
- ☐ Set up discussion forums where experts and novices can discuss issues. In a properly monitored discussion forum, experts do not have to make the same comments over and over again.
- ☐ Have experts critique work by novices. Use online collaboration mechanisms to make the process efficient.
- ☐ Set up a formal telementoring or e-coaching program linking novices with experts in their field.

ACTIVATING SELF-DIRECTED LEARNERS

Many organizations want to make their employees active learners. They mean active in two senses: **actively** pursuing **active** learning experiences. Their goal is to turn passive learners, who learn only what they are told to learn, into active learners, who independently pursue the knowledge they need to do their jobs. This trend is especially important in networked organizations where someone's immediate supervisor may not know enough about the job the employee performs or trends in the employee's field of expertise to recommend training.

For many organizations, the attempt to activate self-directed learners is a culture shift. It does not involve learning specific subject matter but making a change in the way learning is acquired. It requires a fundamental change in the attitude of the learner toward training and those who provide it. Table 7-4 summarizes this change in attitude.

Table 7-4. Change in attitude needed for active learners.

Passive Learner's Attitude		Active Learner's Attitude
My boss will decide what training I need.	→	I will decide what training I need.
The training department will offer the training I need.	→	I will seek and find the training I need.
I learn by listening to or watching an instructor.	→	I learn by actively exploring subjects.

How E-Learning Can Help

E-learning can help activate learners and can help activated learners pursue their individual learning objectives. Learners can proceed at their own pace. A rich navigation model lets learners select the modules they want in the order that makes most sense to them. Online assessments help learners learn what they need to learn, thereby targeting their learning efforts more precisely.

In e-learning, simulations, games, and other interactive experiences make the learning experience an active one. And successful e-learning experiences convince learners that they can learn without the structure of classroom training. E-learning requires and rewards self-motivation.

Economics of Active Learners

The economics of activating learners are not easily calculated, but here are some of the consequences of learners taking responsibility for their own learning:

- Less supervisory time is spent researching training offerings.
- Less time is required for training because activated learners can target their own needs more precisely than can anyone else.
- Learners, knowing their own career goals, can obtain training before moving into a job that requires that training. Such workers are productive over a longer time span.

Using E-Learning to Activate Self-Directed Learners

Use the flexibility and electronic nature of e-learning to enable and encourage learners to adapt training to their individual needs. Here are some productive tactics.

Make Finding Training Easy. Make it easy for potential learners to find the exact e-learning products they need.

- ☐ Publish online course catalogs. These can consolidate courses available from many sources, including individual suppliers, portals, and internal departments.
- ☐ Contract with e-learning portals to make a wide variety of courses available to your learners.
- ☐ Index your learning products. Follow metadata standards (SCORM, IMS, and so forth) to ensure that search engines can find your offerings.

Lead Learners to Independence. Learners with little experience with e-learning or any other form of self-directed learning may need help developing their independent learning skills. Use a progression from instructor-led e-learning to facilitated e-learning and then to self-directed e-learning.

Provide effective instructions on how to use e-learning to customize their learning experiences to meet individual needs. Let learners decide for themselves how to use the materials to accomplish the objectives of the course and their own personal objectives (Duchastel, 1997). Give learners a choice of short courses and a menu of topics within each course. Learners are more successful if the learning is based on their own goals and interests (Schank, 1995).

Have learners monitor their own learning by keeping a learning journal. Every week require learners to submit a list of the most important things they learned that week, what they want to learn more about, and what they still do not understand.

Put Learners in Control. Design the user interface and navigation model so learners control the pace and sequence of their learning experiences. Learners who control their learning experiences commit more fully to them and hence learn more effectively (Soloway et al., 1996). Because learners feel in control, they take more responsibility (McGrath, 1998).

Let learners learn their own way. Give learners a choice of how they master the material and demonstrate mastery. Let them collaborate with others or work alone. Let them take tests or do other kinds of activities.

Let learners set the pace. Let learners participate in synchronized activities, but do not require it. Let individual learners propose their own schedule or work at their own pace as a "class of one."

Help Learners Learn Just What They Need. One of the promises often made for e-learning is that each learner can learn just what he or she needs. Many learners have this expectation. They resent time wasted on material they have no interest in or that they feel they will never apply.

- ☐ Let learners skip material they already know. At least let them take the test on the material at any time.
- ☐ Let advanced learners skip over simple activities. If they fail on the advanced activities, then require them to start over with the simple activities.
- ☐ Keep units short. Provide frequent summaries and activities. Do not require learners to take long segments just to learn a single fact or concept.
- ☐ Provide accurate yet concise previews of units of material so that learners can decide whether to skip the unit, skim it, just read the summary, or take all of it.

INCREASING TRANSFER FROM TRAINING TO WORK

People go to classes, study hard, and pass tests, but often fail to do their jobs better as a result. That is, they don't apply what they learned in training to their jobs or other aspects of their lives. The causes of poor transfer of training to work are complex and manifold. Perhaps learners didn't learn well enough in training, or too much time may have elapsed between training and the need for application. Sometimes they do not recognize cues for application. They may not see practical applications of what they learned or have a desire to apply what they learned. Whatever the reasons, failure to transfer learning to job performance negates the value of training in the first place.

How E-Learning Can Help

E-learning can increase transfer from training to work by making training more closely resemble work and by providing assistance once the learner gets back to work. E-learning can include realistic simulations, case studies, and role-playing activities that prepare learners for the challenges they will encounter in applying the knowledge and skills taught in the course. E-learning can also link to job-related information and tools. Conversely, it can be integrated into information technology tools and into work-flow procedures.

Economics of Transferring Learning to Work

Transfer has a large effect on productivity, a prime concern of Walk the Walk, Inc. Table 7-5 compares two training scenarios Walk the Walk is investigating. Both start with the potential productivity delivered by training. This is the productivity that would occur if everything in training were applied perfectly. For Scenario A, the potential is 100 units per month. For Scenario B, more effective training produces a higher potential of 120 units per month.

This potential is diminished by two factors. The first is the percentage of opportunities recognized. In Scenario A, only half the opportunities are recognized; while in Scenario B, 75 percent are recognized. The second factor is the degree to which workers are successful in applying learning once the opportunity is recognized. For Scenario A, the success rate is 70 percent, but it is 90 percent for Scenario B. The end result is that the workers in Scenario A have a productivity of only 35 units per month compared with a rate of 81 units per month for Scenario B.

Table 7-5. Effect of transfer on productivity.

	Scenario A	Scenario B	
Potential productivity	100	120	units per month
× Opportunities recognized	50%	75%	
× Success applying learning	70%	90%	
= Realized productivity	35	81	units per month

This spreadsheet is available at the book's Website (www.horton.com/using). Try out some variations in this calculation if you wish.

Using E-Learning to Improve Transfer of Training

In considering how e-learning can help learners transfer what they learn into job performance, it is helpful to distinguish among three kinds of transfer: vertical transfer, near transfer, and far transfer. Vertical transfer refers to the ability to integrate component knowledge and skills into higher-level tasks, as, when studying a foreign language, learners use the words they have learned in forming sentences. In near transfer, learners apply knowledge and skills in a way very similar to that in which they were trained. Far transfer, on the other hand, requires applying what was learned to a task quite different from the ones learned and may require analysis and synthesis on the part of the learner.

Vertical Transfer. Vertical transfer involves integrating component knowledge and skills into a whole. Some techniques to improve vertical transfer with e-learning include the following:

☐ Use interactivity, multimedia, and superb instructional design to better teach material in the first place (Bransford, Brown & Cocking, 1999).

☐ Preview the whole while teaching the part. While teaching a component, let learners navigate upward and learn the composite skill.

☐ Teach the part in the context of the whole. Introduce component tasks or skills in the context of the composite task or problem. For example, problem-based learning during the first year of medical school has been found to improve later ability to diagnose medical conditions (Hmelo, 1995).

☐ Contextualize the component task. Use a course map or conceptual map to show how whole and part fit together.

☐ Link component and composite knowledge. Let learners navigate bottom-up or top-down. Provide navigation buttons, summaries, and previews.

Near Transfer. Near transfer requires applying knowledge and skills in conditions similar to those of training. To improve near transfer, broaden the base of training experiences in e-learning so they resemble more work situations. Here are some tips:

☐ Include lots of examples from various fields. Showing a variety of examples that demonstrate the range of applicability of what is being taught helps learners abstract the relevant concepts and characteristics (Gick & Holyoak, 1983). Link to instances, examples, and case studies on the Web.

- ☐ Include lots of practice problems covering cases where knowledge and skills are likely to be applied. Use simple simulations to let learners practice.
- ☐ Generalize case studies and practices. Have learners compose an abstract, write a formula, or present a mathematical model. Highlight aspects of abstract concepts that are relevant to real-world problems (Klahr & Carver, 1988).
- ☐ Give learners checklists and other job aids to prompt application of knowledge. Help learners identify opportunities to apply what they have learned.
- ☐ Convince learners that they will be able to apply the information being taught (Apps, 1991). Show learners potential applications of what they are learning (Anderson, Reder & Simon, 1996).
- ☐ Measure ongoing performance, not just first-day performance. One research study found significantly greater transfer on the second day of performing a skill (Singley & Anderson, 1989).

Far Transfer. The real world is complex, noisy, and messy. Often learners cannot transfer what they learn in a course to the real world because the real world lacks the distinct categories, clear definitions, and simple cases found in training (Harasim, Calvert & Groeneboer, 1997; Jonassen et al., 1997). Far transfer requires applying what was learned to conditions quite different from those of training. Such far transfer may require judgment and creativity on the part of the learner. Here are some tips to enhance far transfer:

- ☐ Require a plan of application. As an ongoing activity, require learners to state specifically how they will apply what they are learning to their jobs. Such an activity provides closure for each major unit. (The "Your Turn" segment of this chapter illustrates this technique.)
- ☐ Require application for graduation. Before awarding the course diploma, require learners to submit examples or stories of how they have applied the content of the course.
- ☐ Make learning more like work. Use case studies and problems based on realistic work situations. Make simulations richly detailed and realistically complex.
- ☐ Use online discussions to provide real-world examples and chances to apply knowledge. Teach collaboration of the type required on the job.
- ☐ Help learners build a support network. Use scavenger hunt activities to have learners identify additional knowledge resources they will use when back on the job. Keep class discussion forums open for several months after training, or transfer class discussions to a job-support forum.

☐ Give learners calculators, expert systems, and other sophisticated job aids aimed at making applying concepts and principles easier.

☐ Make training and its application part of the company's performance appraisal system and part of employees' development plans.

☐ Include self-assessment activities that guide learners to reflect on their learning strategies and how these strategies affect how well they can apply learning on the job (Schonfeld, 1991).

◀◀ ◀◀ ◀◀ ◀◀ ◀◀ ▶▶ ▶▶ ▶▶ ▶▶ ▶▶

YOUR TURN

For at least one of the general learning goals discussed in this chapter, consider how important it is to your organization and how e-learning can help. If you want to perform this activity for multiple goals, photocopy this section or download and print copies from this book's Website (www.horton.com/using). Use worksheet 7-1 to record your answers.

Worksheet 7-1. Accomplishing general learning goals.

1. Pick Your Goal

☐ Getting beginners started

☐ Turning novices into experts

☐ Activating self-directed learners

☐ Increasing transfer from job to work

2. Gauge Its Importance to Your Organization

For how many learners must you accomplish this goal each year?	
How much does your organization spend on this goal each year?	$
What would be the value to your organization if you were perfectly successful accomplishing this goal?	$

3. Identify Ways E-learning Can Help

4. Plan Your Use of E-learning

Action	Person Responsible	Due Date

Section IV:
Reinventing the
Training Function

E-learning does not itself change the role of training or its basic function, but it does provide a prompt, an excuse, and a means for fundamental change in the departments, teams, and organizations that create and conduct training. By removing physical and economic constraints on how we can deliver training, e-learning frees the corporate training function to evolve in new directions.

This section suggests how e-learning may propel training in the following new directions:

- aligning the training department to accomplish organizational goals
- blending e-learning with conventional training
- expanding e-learning courses to create complete learning environments.

In this section, trainers and their managers will find opportunities to better serve their organizations while sculpting vital new careers.

8

Rethinking the Training Department

E-learning offers an opportunity to "rewire" the training department, revamp its image, align it with organizational goals, and perhaps transform it into a profit center. None of these changes occurs automatically with e-learning. In fact, some of these changes do not require e-learning at all. E-learning does, however, provide the obvious opportunity to do things differently.

REVAMPING TRAINING'S IMAGE

Negative stereotypes of training departments and trainers stigmatize all involved in delivering training. Such images, perhaps decades out of date, are pervasive in many organizations.

How Is Training Viewed in Your Organization?

How do the managers, executives, staff, suppliers, and customers of your organization view the training department? How do they talk about you when you are not present? Well, here are some statements made about trainers and training organizations over the past few years:

- "They're like a baby with a hammer. Their solution to everything is another course, another course, another course."
- "They're technophobic. I see why it took 30 years to get overhead projectors from the bowling alleys into the classroom."
- "Those who can, do; those who cannot, teach."
- "A world unto themselves. They have no concern for what the rest of the company is trying to accomplish. I don't think they ever heard of a budget."

- "All they want to do is sit around and debate educational theories and write white papers on how to build a learning organization. We need training now!"
- "They're OK for the touchy-feely stuff that nobody really needs, but we go outside for hard business and technical training."
- "A bunch of wannabe stand-up comedians and actors. They're just in it for the audience. Everybody wants to be the sage on a stage."

Many think training is not important and that its offerings are irrelevant, out of date, or ineffective. Many executives see training only as an expense—a necessary expense—but an expense nonetheless.

Some training departments do deserve bad reputations, but most deserve a better reputation than they have. E-learning may be a way to get people to take a fresh look at the department and judge it for what it can do for the organization as a whole.

How E-Learning Can Revamp Training's Image

The transition to e-learning affords lots of opportunities to shed outworn stereotypes and invite a new appraisal. Draw on the change in techniques used to deliver training as an excuse to makeover the training department's image. Here are some suggestions:

- ☐ Innovate, innovate, innovate. Do things differently. Try new ideas. Make clear that you are not satisfied replicating your classroom offerings over the Web. Don't just Webcast lectures or dump training manuals online. Develop highly interactive simulations and things no one has done yet.
- ☐ Use e-learning to catch management's attention. Issue frequent reports. Invite executives to "private screenings."
- ☐ Make clear the business purposes of everything you do. State the business goals of all e-learning projects. Reveal business results.
- ☐ Give the department a new identity. Create a colorful logo for the department and for early e-learning projects. Plaster it everywhere: on posters, coffee mugs, pencils, screen savers, splash screens, t-shirts, ties, and scarves.
- ☐ Publicize your e-learning efforts. Use all the standard publicity techniques, such as press releases, case studies, and interviews. Publish inside your company through newsletters and closed-circuit TV channels, and intranet sites.
- ☐ Premier your efforts with a bang. Put a countdown timer on your department Website. Hold a big announcement meeting. Conduct brown-bag luncheons to explain the program. Get "face-time" wherever you can.

ALIGNING TRAINING WITH ORGANIZATIONAL GOALS

Throughout the world, training organizations are trying to align their efforts with organizational goals rather than to the abstract goals of education or the private preferences of the training department itself. With goals aligned, training swims in the fast, clear currents of the mainstream, not the stagnant, muddy backwaters.

The reasons for such a retargeting of training efforts range from the ethical to the pragmatic. Some argue that it is unethical for training departments to pursue goals other than those of the larger organization from which they receive funding. And this service of organizational needs helps justify the funding and increases in that funding as well. Alignment with organizational goals also demolishes the stereotype of the ivory-tower training department, aloof from the real-world business of the organization.

Such an alignment with business goals can better support development plans for employees by human resources and other departments. It can tie into competency development and succession planning projects. Each new e-learning project can be tagged to specific development objectives.

How to Align Training with Organizational Goals

To align training with organizational goals, clearly identify the goals of your organization and focus the efforts of training on meeting those goals.

First, learn what are the real business and social goals, not just the ones featured in the annual report or on posters in headquarters. Look at what efforts get noticed, praised, and funded.

Identify true training needs. Do not limit your research to those who currently take classroom training. Seek out those at distant offices, those who took one class but never a second class, and departments that take fewer than the average number of classes. In conducting your research, do not make the mistake of using only online surveys.

Invite review of your projects by executives and key managers. If you can do so without compromising security, include customers and perhaps community members. Conduct reviews early enough that you can make changes. At least have project objectives reviewed.

Focus on finding solutions to organizational problems, not just more applications

> ### What Are Worthy Organizational Goals?
>
> **O**rganizational goals tend to be of two types. Some are direct business goals and concern the profitability of the organization. If a hostile takeover is threatened, you had better focus on these goals. Social goals concern how the organization relates to outside organizations and people. Social goals appeal to altruism and conscience. They are also important for public relations if your company sells tobacco, has been adjudicated a predatory monopoly, or has just run its supertanker aground in a wildlife sanctuary. Table 8-1 lists some worthy organizational and social goals.

for training courses. Consider all options: classroom training, e-learning, blends, outside consultants, university extensions, junior colleges, training portals, conferences, books, and newsletters. Involve other departments in developing solutions that go beyond training.

Anchor all training projects on business objectives. Require each training project to explicitly state its intended business goals and estimate its return-on-investment. Follow up each project with a high-level evaluation that determines whether the project met its business goals.

Table 8-1. Organizational and social goals.

Organizational Goals	Social Goals
Increase profits, revenues, market share, margin, stock price, and other standard measures of business success.	Enhance philanthropic image.
	Make your company's products and services appear to have great value to society.
Better recruit and retain talented individuals.	
	Be recognized as a good neighbor in the communities where your organization is active.
Bring products to market quicker.	
Improve customer service and product quality.	Turn greener. Appear more environmentally responsible.
Cut costs, waste, and idle time.	

How E-Learning Helps Align with Organizational Goals

E-learning does not itself align anything, but it can provide the catalyst to make fundamental changes in the ways projects are chartered and evaluated.

Because e-learning is new, it may be easier to get management's attention, especially for projects based on technologies reported extensively in the business press and even in the evening news. An e-learning project represents a credible justification for a new start.

The "e" in e-learning stands for "electronic," and that simplifies the effort required to demonstrate alignment of training to organizational efforts. Because everything about e-learning can be done online, it is visible to everyone on the network. Such openness reduces misunderstandings about the mission of the project.

With e-learning, much of the tracking of results can be built in and automated. You often can track performance back on the job using the same technologies as for e-learning.

For information technology companies, e-learning naturally aligns with other information products or information-technology projects.

Starting with Business Goals

Successful projects need worthy business goals. Such business goals should guide decision making at all levels. In many cases, however, the training department is not involved in a project until after the general business goals are set. Ascertaining the project's underlying business goals may be more a matter of organizational archaeology than forward planning. Nevertheless, knowing the business goals is essential to proceeding on a training project.

The Cascade of Goals. For success, a training project should be able to trace its goal back to valuable and recognized business goals. Doing so requires understanding the cascade of dependencies linking business goals to learning goals. Figure 8-1 shows this cascade.

Figure 8-1. Cascade of business, performance, and training goals.

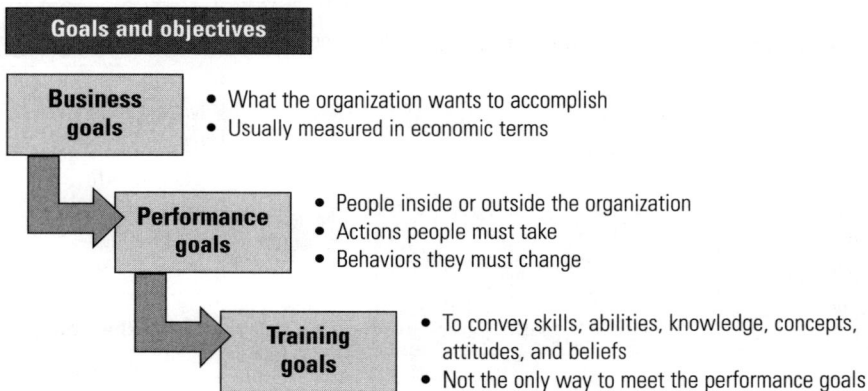

Goals and objectives

Business goals
- What the organization wants to accomplish
- Usually measured in economic terms

Performance goals
- People inside or outside the organization
- Actions people must take
- Behaviors they must change

Training goals
- To convey skills, abilities, knowledge, concepts, attitudes, and beliefs
- Not the only way to meet the performance goals

First are the business goals. These state what the organization wants to accomplish. Business goals are usually stated in economic terms, such as the profit the company wants to make, costs it wants to cut, the market share it hopes to achieve, or the return it promises its stockholders.

Next come the performance goals, which state what must happen for the business goals to be met. Performance goals concern people and what they must do. These people may be inside the organization (employees) or outside the organization (customers). Performance goals specify exactly what actions they must take or what behaviors they must change.

The third tier in the cascade contains the training goals. The training goals specify what the training must accomplish. Training goals can include the skills, abilities, concepts, attitudes, and beliefs the training is to convey.

Keep in mind that your training project may not be the only one aimed at accomplishing the performance goals. Other initiatives may be striving to accomplish or assist in accomplishing the same performance goals as your project. You must be aware of these projects and what they will contribute.

Basing Other Goals on the Business Goal. Consider how the goal for a training project can derive from a business goal and how other goals may be involved as well. Figure 8-2 shows the goals for a training project. This project of developing a course for a management consulting group on reading Gantt charts started by interviewing managers of the company to learn the underlying business reasons they wanted to develop such a course. Managers revealed that their business goal was to increase their consulting and training revenues by 50 percent over the next couple of years.

Figure 8-2. Goals for a training project.

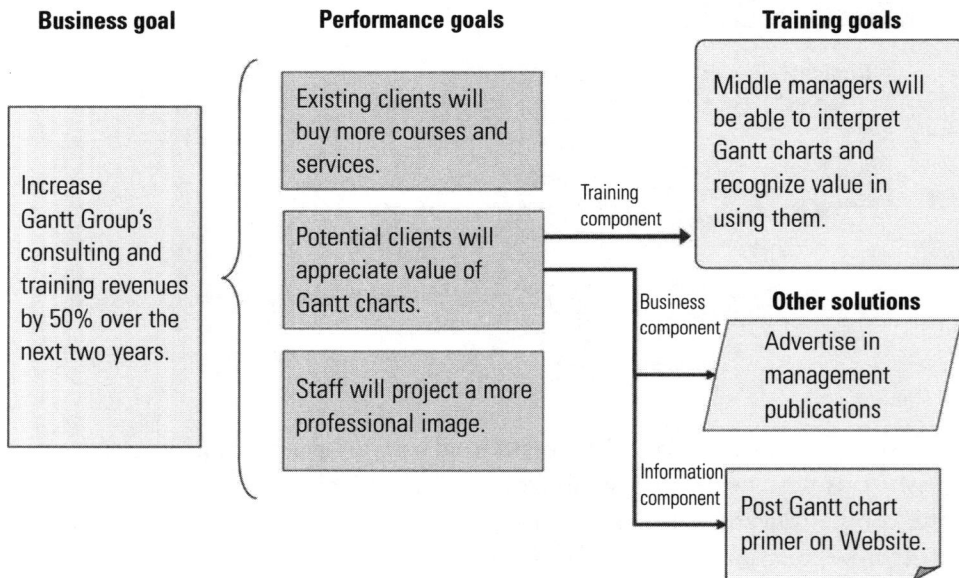

Business goal	Performance goals	Training goals
Increase Gantt Group's consulting and training revenues by 50% over the next two years.	Existing clients will buy more courses and services.	Middle managers will be able to interpret Gantt charts and recognize value in using them.
	Potential clients will appreciate value of Gantt charts.	
	Staff will project a more professional image.	

Training component → Middle managers will be able to interpret Gantt charts and recognize value in using them.

Business component → **Other solutions**
Advertise in management publications

Information component → Post Gantt chart primer on Website.

To that end, they had identified three things that must happen. Though they did not identify them as such, these three intermediate goals were performance goals. The first was that existing clients would buy more of the firm's classroom courses and consulting services. The second performance goal was that potential clients would appreciate the value of Gantt charts to them in their business and thereby see the value in the kinds of training and services offered by the firm. It was this goal that gave rise to this project. A third performance goal was that the staff of the firm would project a more professional image.

134

These three performance goals had their own initiatives to accomplish the goal. Now look at the initiatives for the second goal. The first initiative was to teach middle managers to interpret Gantt charts and recognize the value in using them. This was the training component of meeting the performance goal.

Other solutions were to be pursued in parallel with the training. These included advertising in management publications (a business component) and posting a primer on Gantt charts on the corporation's Website (an information component).

This kind of analysis can reveal what a project is to accomplish and how it fits into a matrix of related efforts.

Evaluating Against Business Goals

Just setting goals is hardly sufficient. You must follow up with evaluations that align with the goals set at the beginning of the project. As figure 8-3 shows, each level of evaluation corresponds to one level of goals.

Figure 8-3. Levels of evaluation match levels of goals.

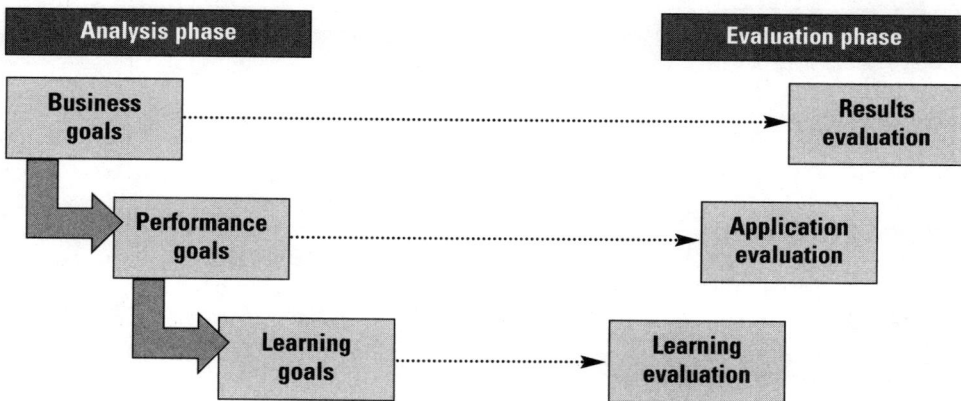

The process of evaluating e-learning is covered in the book *Evaluating E-Learning* by the same author and publisher as this book.

BECOMING A PROFIT CENTER

Chapter 4 considered the ways that selling e-learning could contribute to corporate revenues. There the focus was on selling to outside organizations and individuals. This chapter explores the prospects of selling internally by turning the training department into a profit center.

Making the training department a profit center means that it pays its own way. Such an economically independent training department must finance its own activities by selling products and services. It typically sells to other departments within the organization by budget transfers or "funny money."

The concept of a profit center may be expanded to allow the internal department to sell its offerings to outside organizations. There is little new in this because training departments commonly provide customer training. A more important change occurs when the training department loses its monopoly on internal training, as other departments are free to buy their training from the training department or from other sources. As a profit center, the training department must operate as a business competing for customers and striving for a profit.

Why Make Training a Profit Center?

The reasons for making training a profit center depend on one's perspective. Table 8-2 contains some commonly cited reasons.

Table 8-2. Common reasons for making the training department a profit center.

From Viewpoint of the Training Department	From Viewpoint of the Larger Organization
Demonstrate the value of training to the company and to other departments.	Create a new business unit contributing revenue to the company.
Demonstrate understanding of business.	Prepare the training department to be spun off.
Generate revenue by outside sales.	Require understanding of business processes by the training department leadership and staff.
Let the market set priorities.	Use marketplace economics to efficiently allocate resources to areas that need training.
Obtain more autonomy and authority to make business decisions.	
Experience the challenge and satisfaction of running a business.	

What Does E-Learning Contribute to Profit?

E-learning offers a valid excuse for reworking the economics of the training department. It is sufficiently different, and its costs are accounted in such a distinct way that new accounting procedures may be needed anyway. Why not go the rest of the way and make training a profit center?

E-learning offers well-defined products and services that are clearly intellectual property. E-learning products can be marketed in several ways: as multicourse certificate programs, as single courses, as mini-courses, and as micro-courses. Offerings can be blended with classroom learning. Modular e-learning can be mixed and matched to fill niche needs.

The economics of e-learning reward good business practices. Because e-learning has low delivery costs (no travel by instructors, no shipping, automated registration), the more people you train, the more money you make.

What Is Your Market?

What are the markets for a training department functioning as a profit center? Take a look at some potential sources of revenue.

☐ *Internal employees who currently take classroom training:* If e-learning can be made less expensive and more convenient, some classroom learners may prefer e-learning. Such a switch may, of course, lessen revenues from classroom training.

☐ *Internal employees who do not take classroom training:* E-learning can find a market among those who are too busy for classroom training, who travel too much to meet a classroom schedule, who cannot afford travel and other expenses. Chapter 6 lists these groups and suggests ways e-learning can meet their needs.

☐ *Internal employees taking courses from outside suppliers:* Can you create or find a better course? Can you customize the course? Could you negotiate a better price?

☐ *Internal employees who need customized versions of external courses:* Can you skinny down the courses, add custom content, link to reference materials, add assessments tailored to your needs, and link assessments to internal systems?

☐ *External learners:* The training center functioning as a profit center can market to the same external customers identified in Chapter 4, namely, users of your company's product or service, third-party trainers, those who sell your product, suppliers to your company, and others in your industry.

Workers are demanding more training of the type e-learning can deliver. A survey conducted by the Gallup Organization found that 99 percent of workers felt they needed additional training and that they strongly preferred informal on-job training and self-paced training to formal classroom training (Schaaf, 1998).

Economic Model of a Training Profit Center

As a profit center, the training department needs a sound economic model that explains how and when it will make a profit. Table 8-3 shows a simplified model of the first five years of operations as a profit center based on selling e-learning products. Notice a couple of points about this model. Because of the costs of initially developing e-learning, the profit center runs up a loss in its first year and only breaks even the second year. It is not until the fourth year that its revenues are sufficient to pay back the loss. This means that the organization must subsidize the startup for the profit center. This subsidy may be a one-time grant or a no-interest loan. Or the training department might use revenues from classroom offerings to pay for the costs of getting started with e-learning. As you can see, training departments face the same financial difficulties as any start-up business.

Table 8-3. Economic model for a profit center.

	Year 1	Year 2	Year 3	Year 4	Year 5
Revenue					
Internal charge backs	$200	$300	$400	$500	$500
External sales	$300	$350	$400	$450	$500
Total revenue	$500	$650	$800	$950	$1,000
Expenses					
Developing e-learning	$1,000	$500	$200	$200	$200
Conducting e-learning	$150	$150	$150	$150	$150
Total costs	$1,150	$650	$350	$350	$350
Net Profit	− $650	$0	$450	$600	$650
Cumulative profit	− $650	− $650	− $200	$400	$1,050

Note: All figures in $1000s.

The Critical Issue of Subsidies

The economics of a profit center depend greatly on whether any of its costs are subsidized or paid for by the organization as a whole. In estimating the profitability of a profit center, begin by asking whether there are any costs that the department does not have to pay? These may include the costs of offices, furniture, network connections, and computers. They may also include general benefits such as access to the company gym or day-care center.

You can download this model from this book's Website (www.horton.com/using). Try some variations, such as spreading out the costs of developing e-learning or adding costs and revenues for classroom training efforts into the model.

Marketing Internally

Marketing is required regardless of whether the department is a profit center or not. Marketing is more easily justified in the case of a profit center where additional sales of e-learning products generate additional profits. Here are just a few ways to promote your e-learning offerings within your company:

- ☐ email broadcasts to employees whom you have identified as needing training
- ☐ ads and articles in the company newsletter
- ☐ presentations as part of new-hire orientation classes
- ☐ flyers in new-hire packets
- ☐ ads and features on the company TV network
- ☐ posters, mugs, pencils, t-shirts, and other items given to trainees and new employees
- ☐ an internal intranet site and forums on internal newsgroups
- ☐ lobbying human resources to include your training in the development plans for all employees.

◀◀ ◀◀ ◀◀ ◀◀ ◀◀ ▶▶ ▶▶ ▶▶ ▶▶ ▶▶

YOUR TURN

Ready to rethink your training department? Use this activity to guide your thoughts—and actions.

Revamp Your Image

Identify four negative perceptions about your training efforts and list ways you can use e-learning to reverse these perceptions. Enter your answers on worksheet 8-1.

Worksheet 8-1. Reversing negative perceptions about training.	
Negative Perception	**How I Can Use E-learning to Reverse This Perception**

Align Training with Organizational Goals

Pick a training project and show how its goals derive from high-level organizational goals.

1. List your main business goal. What does the business want to accomplish?
2. Derive the performance goals necessary to accomplish that business goal. Who must do what in order for the organization to meet the business goal?
3. Pick the one performance goal that your project aims to accomplish.
4. Set the training goal for your project. What must it teach? To whom?
5. List other solutions necessary to accomplish the performance goal you have chosen.

Enter your answers on worksheet 8-2.

Worksheet 8-2. Translating business goals to training goals.		
Business Goal	**Performance Goals**	**Training Goals**
What does the business want to accomplish?	To meet the business goal, who must do what?	What must your training accomplish to ensure the performance goal is met?
		Other Solutions

Turn Your Department into a Profit Center

If you work in an internal training department, imagine that you want to make it a profit center. Use worksheet 8-3 to define your plan.

Worksheet 8-3. Turning your department into a profit center.

1. Identify Reasons to Make Your Department a Profit Center

2. Identify Markets for Your E-Learning Products

Market	How will you promote your offerings in this market?

3. Establish Your Economic Model

Specify how your department will make money selling e-learning. Show the financial results for the first few years.

	Year 1	Year 2	Year 3	Year 4	Year 5
Revenue					
Internal charge backs	$	$	$	$	$
External sales	$	$	$	$	$
Total revenue	$	$	$	$	$
Expenses					
Developing e-learning	$	$	$	$	$
Conducting e-learning	$	$	$	$	$
Total expenses	$	$	$	$	$
Net Profit	$	$	$	$	$
Cumulative profit	$	$	$	$	$

9

Blending E-Learning and Classroom Training

Contrary to popular perceptions, e-learning and classroom training are more yin and yang than sworn enemies. Many projects for the foreseeable future can productively combine these two forms.

WHY BLEND CLASSROOM TRAINING AND E-LEARNING?

Blending attempts to combine the best features of classroom training with the best features of e-learning. Table 9-1 lists desirable characteristics of each form of training.

Table 9-1. Desirable characteristics of classroom training and e-learning.

Classroom Training	E-learning
Familiarity to learners and instructors.	Excitement of something new.
Ability to handle subjects requiring face-to-face contact.	Ability to span distances, reducing travel required.
Low up-front costs and rapid development.	Efficiency in delivering routine subjects.

Blending can leverage the desirable characteristics of one form of training to motivate learners to do well in the other. For example, Sun Microsystems requires new sales representatives to take and pass an e-learning course before they can attend a weeklong classroom course in California (Densford, 1998).

Blending also provides learners and instructors a smoother transition as they move from traditional classroom training to pure, self-directed e-learning. It provides a safety net to ensure that no one gets lost in the transition.

Guest Editorial: Blending Is a Sham

Blending is noise on the radar screen of progress, nothing more. You should ignore it and continue full speed ahead. Let me list reasons why.

First, imagine you are attending a medical convention. At this convention you hear a presentation announcing a breakthrough technique that is 100 percent successful in increasing human life span. In fact, there is perfect statistical correlation between the degree to which the technique is practiced and health. Those who failed to practice this technique all died. (Glad you weren't in that control group, eh?) You'd be intrigued, excited, and ready to adopt the technique, right? At the end of the presentation, you learn that the technique is called "breathing." How would you feel? You should feel the same way about blending, because it is nothing new. You have been doing it all your (learning) life. Can you think of anything you learned by just one medium, one technique, or one method alone? "Blending" changes nothing. The mix of learning experiences has continually evolved since Neanderthals combined grunting and pointing.

Second, the propaganda of the radical *blendistas* would have us believe that the only possible blends are alternating swatches of classroom and online learning. The result is a less diverse training mix, because purist blending ignores other combinations and novel approaches. True blending (which is what has existed all along) would include books, magazines, online documents, Websites, job aids, Internet newsgroups, mentors, study groups, and many other knowledge sources in the mix.

Third, the promise of blending is not always realized. Instead of getting the best of classroom training and the best of e-learning, many blends combine the fixed schedule and batch-manufacturing mentality of classroom training with the crudeness of early-generation e-learning.

Fourth, blending gives neo-Luddite instructors and managers an excuse to maintain the status quo. The position of "sage on the stage" is safe. The training center still looms large on the corporate skyline. Instead of building halfway houses for classroom junkies, we should get on with the job of building great e-learning and leave classrooms to do what they do so very well.

Fifth, blending diverts attention, talent, funding, and energy from the task of developing highly effective e-learning and deploying it widely. Does anyone claim they have perfected e-learning yet? If not, then how can they accurately predict its full potential alone, much less in a blend?

The best way to blend is to forget about "blending" and just design the most effective training solutions we can.

Thorndon Killabit

COMMON FORMS OF BLENDING

For many, the term *blending* means little more than marching learners through a curriculum containing both classroom and e-learning courses. Merely alternating courses is only one way that blending can occur. Here are some other ways open-minded designers are combining e-learning and classroom training.

Sandwiches

Instead of serving doughnuts and coffee, serve sandwiches—learning sandwiches, that is. These are learning sequences that alternate classroom training and e-learning. Figure 9-1 shows two popular entrées on the learning sandwich menu.

Figure 9-1. Popular forms of learning sandwiches.

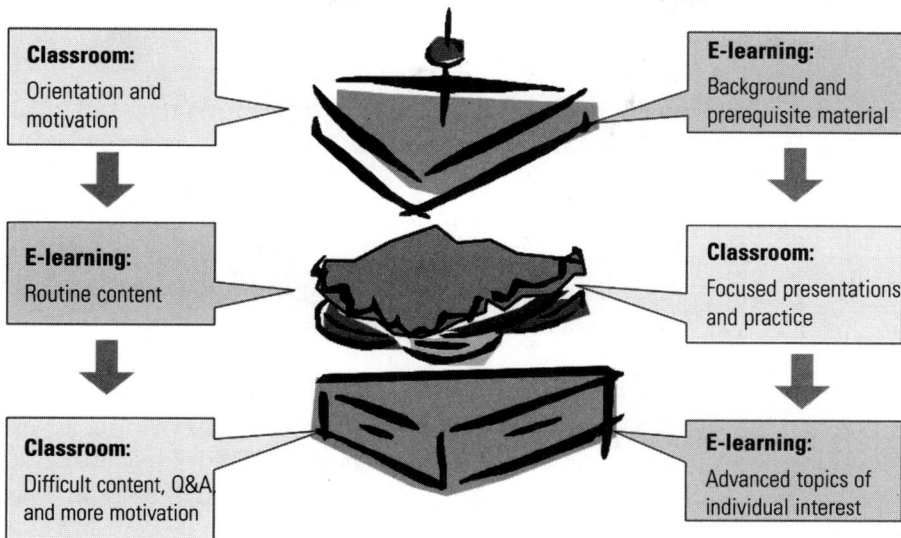

Classroom: Orientation and motivation	**E-learning:** Background and prerequisite material
E-learning: Routine content	**Classroom:** Focused presentations and practice
Classroom: Difficult content, Q&A and more motivation	**E-learning:** Advanced topics of individual interest

Classroom/E-Learning/Classroom Sandwich. One learning sandwich might begin with an orientation and motivation in a classroom setting, followed by e-learning for routine content, and conclude with classroom meetings to cover difficult content, answer learners' questions, and provide extra motivation. Such a sandwich would be appropriate for novices learning routine but difficult matter, especially if the learners have little e-learning experience.

E-Learning/Classroom/E-Learning Sandwich. The opposite structure might work for building expertise among learners already comfortable with e-learning. These learners might start in e-learning to brush up on prerequisite material and round out background knowledge. These e-learning sessions would prepare them for highly efficient and focused activities in a classroom setting. Optional advanced topics might be available afterward by e-learning.

Such a structure works well for advanced subjects taken by a variety of learners who have different backgrounds and goals but all need the same core of face-to-face learning.

Embedding E-Learning in Classroom Training

Some blends are primarily one form of training with elements of the other form embedded within it. You can produce this kind of blend by introducing elements of e-learning into a traditional classroom course and by using e-learning technologies to perform routine activities associated with classroom training. Here are some aspects of e-learning that classroom instructors are using today:

- [ ] Learners submit homework by email or to a discussion forum.
- [ ] Announcements are made via a discussion forum or email.
- [ ] High-quality multimedia presentations convey routine material.
- [ ] A class discussion forum lets learners continue conversations among themselves and with the instructor after class.
- [ ] "Office hours" are conducted by instant messaging and videoconferencing, as well as by phone and an open office door.
- [ ] Study groups meet using online conferencing and collaboration tools.
- [ ] Reading assignments include Web-based materials.

Such an approach gently prepares learners and instructors to make the leap to true e-learning. It makes classroom training more efficient by making outside-the-classroom communications possible among widely distributed learners. It also provides a way to test and to re-use e-learning assets such as multimedia presentations.

Embedding Classroom Training in E-Learning

Getting started in e-learning should not feel like you've been whisked aboard an alien spaceship. One way to reduce the shock of e-learning's newness is to let learners bring along some of their favorite parts of the classroom experience. Table 9-2 lists some treasured aspects of classroom training and how they can be embedded (or at least emulated) in an e-learning course.

Table 9-2. Emulating valuable aspects of classroom training in e-learning.

Aspect of Classroom Training	How It Can Be Embedded in E-learning
Warm greeting from the instructor.	Recorded greeting in video or audio.
Ability to ask questions.	Email address of a facilitator, link to a discussion forum, or just a telephone number.
Well-done lectures and stories.	Recorded presentations, stories, demonstrations, speeches for playback.
Encouragement of fellow learners.	Ongoing discussion among all learners currently enrolled in the course.
Help getting oriented.	Optional get-together meeting for learners who will be taking e-learning.

Embedding aspects of classroom training in e-learning is a good strategy when learners may be apprehensive about e-learning or need a safety net of human support.

Electronic Drop-Ins in Classroom Training

Some training organizations are increasing enrollment in their classroom courses by using Internet collaboration mechanisms to let distant learners virtually sit in on classroom courses. The goal is to enable remote learners to participate in training without having to travel to the site and without having to develop new forms of training. Here's how it might work.

Ahead of time, remote learners receive copies of slides, handouts, and other materials that will be used in the classroom. They then have the option of printing out these materials or just following along on their computer screens.

Streaming video and audio are used to let remote learners see and hear what is done and said in the classroom. A camera may be fixed on the podium or stage where the instructor speaks and demonstrates ideas. In a more sophisticated setup, multiple cameras are used, and a cameraman switches among views of the presenter, slides, other materials being discussed, and the classroom audience. Usually a second microphone is positioned to capture questions and comments from learners in the classroom.

Remote learners ask questions by sending email to a designated address or by typing messages into an instant messaging window. To keep the instructor from being distracted, questions are typically screened by an assistant, who then asks them aloud so everyone can hear the question and answer.

No one would claim that the experience of the remote learner is as rich and effective as that of the person physically in the classroom. But such an experience can still lead to effective learning, especially for learners who have the motivation to learn but not the time or money to travel to the site of training.

Virtual Classrooms

The virtual classroom approach blends structure of classroom training with the technology and media of e-learning. It uses traditional classroom training as a metaphor to organize e-learning in a way that makes it familiar to learners and instructors, thereby preserving some of its key advantages.

In the virtual classroom, each aspect of e-learning is modeled on a part of classroom training. It may have the same name as the classroom training and may be represented by an emblem or visual image that mimics its appearance in the classroom. Table 9-3 illustrates these correspondences.

The virtual classroom approach is good for moving proven classroom courses to e-learning when there is not time to retrain instructors or create new material.

Table 9-3. Virtual classroom replicates aspects of real classroom.

Part of Classroom Training	How Implemented in a Virtual Classroom
Instructor.	Facilitator, supplemented with recorded presentations, demonstrations, speeches, stories.
Class of learners.	Learners are assigned to a class that consists of a limited number of others taking the course at the same time and pace. Learners in the class can contact one another through a discussion forum or instant messaging.
Paper handouts.	Handouts available for download from the course's Webpage. Handouts are in HTML for reading off the screen or Adobe Acrobat PDF for printing.
Asking questions of the instructor.	During live presentations, learners can "raise their hands," using that feature in collaboration software, or just type into an open instant messaging window.
Team projects.	Groups of learners collaborate on an assignment using a special thread in the discussion forum and instant messaging. Their result is posted to the forum where the instructor and other learners can see and critique it.
Study groups.	Learners meet on discussion threads or in chat rooms to compare notes, discuss material, or just socialize.

ECONOMICS OF BLENDING

Blending, not surprisingly, combines the cost structures of classroom training and e-learning. Table 9-4 shows a cost estimate for a three-year training program implemented as classroom training, as self-directed e-learning, and as a blend of the two forms. The total costs for the blended solution are midway between those for the two pure forms.

Perhaps you would like to try to make the blend more economical. Other ways of blending may indeed offer different economics. Download the spreadsheet from this book's Website (www.horton.com/using) and try out some different assumptions.

TOWARD A STRATEGY FOR BLENDING

Blending is too new to have clear-cut rules or guaranteed step-by-step procedures. At this stage, the best bet is to follow this strategy for making the key decisions necessary to invent a blending solution. The three main steps are:

1. Divide the subject into logical chunks.
2. Decide what form of training to use for each chunk.
3. Decide how to combine the chunks in the best blend.

The following sections cover these steps and provide an example of deciding a blending strategy for a complex subject.

	Instructor-led Classroom Training	Self-directed E-learning	Blended E-learning and Classroom Training	
Table 9-4. Economics of pure and blended forms of training.				
Assumptions				
Life span of course	3	3	3	years
Learners per year	200	200	200	learners per year
Class size	20	0	20	learners per class
Classes (offerings)	30	0	30	offerings
Costs				
One-time Costs				
Course development	$50,000	$300,000	$150,000	per course
Per Offering Costs				
Instructor costs	$1,500	$0	$800	per offering
Classroom rental	$1,200	$0	$600	per offering
= Total per offering	$2,700	$0	$1,400	per offering
× Number of offerings	30	0	30	offerings
= Total offering costs	$81,000	$0	$42,000	per course
Per Learner Costs				
Travel	$800	$0	$500	per learner
Time away from job	$800	$200	$400	per learner
Technical support	$0	$200	$0	per learner
= Total per-learner costs	$1,600	$400	$900	per learner
× Number of learners	600	600	600	learners
= Total learner costs	$960,000	$240,000	$540,000	per course
Total Costs	$1,091,000	$540,000	$732,000	per course

Step 1: Dividing into Logical Chunks

The first step in designing a blended training solution is to divide the subject into logical chunks. There are several cleavage planes you can use to divide the overall subject.

- *Current courses:* If you are assembling a curriculum by purchasing or combining existing courses, you may chose to divide the subject up into units represented by those existing courses. You can then just mix the available classroom and e-learning courses as appropriate.
- *Materials used now:* If you are converting existing courses, you may be loath to replace materials that have proven themselves, especially if such materials can easily be converted for use in e-learning.

■ *Learning experiences:* The things done to trigger learning experiences often cannot be divided. Instead, identify key experiences that enable learning, especially important ideas, and group these with the necessary supporting activities and experiences.

■ *Components useful in future courses:* If you are developing modular training, consider what chunks might be useful in future courses or blends. Group these components so they can be developed as reusable modules.

Step 2: Deciding Which Form to Use

To decide what form of training to use for each component you have identified, consider issues such as the economics of development and deployment, pedagogy and instructional design, technological constraints, and the psychology of the learner. Table 9-5 provides some guidance.

Table 9-5. Issues in deciding what form of training to use.

Issue	If ...	Then Use...
Economics	Little time or money to develop.	Classroom
	Available off the shelf as e-learning.	E-learning
	Material changes often.	E-learning
	Content is in electronic form.	E-learning
Pedagogy	Material is same for everybody.	E-learning
	Face-to-face contact required.	Classroom
	No experience with e-learning.	Classroom
Technology	Learners lack computers or network connections.	Classroom
	Material requires multimedia to explain.	E-learning
Psychology	Learners not highly motivated.	Classroom
	Learners self-motivated.	E-learning

Step 3: Deciding How to Combine Components

Earlier you saw several different ways of blending e-learning and classroom training. Three general ways of combining the two forms follow:

■ *Alternate:* Present complete units entirely in one form followed by complete units in a distinctly different form.

■ *Embed components:* Most training is provided by one form. Within that form occur small units of other forms.

■ *Mix components:* Units of training mix components of different forms freely.

Example of Blending a Subject

Now step through an example of deciding how to use blending for a moderately complex course. Don't Make Me Come Back There, Inc., teaches courses in conflict resolution. They offer a course for new supervisors on how to resolve disputes between subordinates.

How might a blended approach work for this course?

Step 1: Dividing the Subject. The first step is to decompose the skill into its components. Ask yourself these questions: What skill are you teaching? To whom are you teaching the skill?

In order to acquire the skill, what must learners know, feel, believe, and be able to do? Figure 9-2 shows the answers to these questions for the example case. The numbers beside items do not indicate priority or sequence. They are to help track these items through subsequent phases of design.

What must new supervisors learn in order to handle disputes among subordinates? First, you may want to give them a procedure to follow to resolve disputes. You may also want them to know some calming words to use instead of inflammatory words in conversations with agitated subordinates.

What attitudes must a supervisor possess in order to successfully resolve disputes? Openness to the opinions and ideas of subordinates would help, as would calmness in the middle of a heated conversation.

And, unless supervisors believe that disputes can be destructive, they will not be motivated to intervene to resolve them. Finally, supervisors must be able to listen objectively.

Figure 9-2. Goals for the example course.

In order to apply this skill: *RESOLVE DISPUTES BETWEEN SUBORDINATES* ,
this group of learners: *NEW SUPERVISORS* , **must:**

Know:	Believe that:
1. *PROCEDURE FOR RESOLVING DISPUTES*	5. *DISPUTES ARE DESTRUCTIVE*
2. *CALMING WORDS*	

Have these attitudes:	Be able to:
3. *OPENNESS*	6. *LISTEN OBJECTIVELY*
4. *CALMNESS*	

Step 2: Deciding What Learning Experiences to Use for Each. Now that you have identified what you must teach, ask what experience best teaches that fact, belief, attitude, or sub-skill? At this stage you are not asking what form of training to use, just what human experience best teaches the required item. You will later decide what form best produces that human experience. Figure 9-3 shows an inventory of what must be learned and how each item might best be learned.

Perhaps you decide that the procedure for resolving disputes should be memorized so that it can be recalled reliably in the presence of stress. This also applies to the calming words used in such conversations.

Figure 9-3. Learning experiences to teach each component.

What experience best teaches each fact, belief, attitude, and sub-skill?

What must be learned:	How best learned:
1. PROCEDURE FOR RESOLVING DISPUTES	MEMORIZE AND PRACTICE
2. CALMING WORDS	MEMORIZE AND PRACTICE
3. OPENNESS	GROUP CRITIQUE AND PRACTICE
4. CALMNESS	SIMULATED CONFRONTATIONS
5. DISPUTES ARE DESTRUCTIVE	CASE STUDIES
6. LISTEN OBJECTIVELY	ROLE-PLAYING AND PRACTICE

Openness is tougher. It may take observation and critique by a group of the supervisor's peers. And it may require repeated practice.

Calmness may require desensitizing the supervisor to the angry words and insults of others. You may decide, for the purpose of this example, that the best way to desensitize the supervisor is through simulated confrontations.

To persuade the supervisor that disputes should be resolved and not ignored, you may choose to have the supervisor experience a series of case studies showing how in situations like those the supervisor will experience, failure to resolve disputes cost the supervisor and the supervisor's organization dearly.

Listening skills may be honed through a role-playing activity.

Now you can begin to think about the best way to convey each fact, belief, attitude, or sub-skill. In analyzing each, ask whether it requires a person other than the learner? And if it does, must the contact be face-to-face? Then—and only then—can you decide the best way to deliver that component of training. Figure 9-4 shows some decisions regarding the items you must teach.

Figure 9-4. Best way to instigate the required learning experiences.

What must be learned:	Requires person?	Requires F2F	How to deliver it:
1. PROCEDURE FOR RESOLVING DISPUTES	–	–	WEB OR BOOK
2. CALMING WORDS	–	–	WEB OR BOOK
3. OPENNESS	✔	✔	CLASSROOM
4. CALMNESS	✔	✔	CLASSROOM
5. DISPUTES ARE DESTRUCTIVE	–	–	WEB
6. LISTEN OBJECTIVELY	✔	–	WEB OR CLASSROOM

You decided that the procedure for resolving disputes needed to be memorized. Adults seldom need another person to help them memorize a simple list. For memorization activities, the Web or a book would be more than adequate. The same reasoning applies to the list of calming words.

Learning openness requires group critique by other human beings. Because openness is signaled by tone of voice as well as subtle aspects of facial expressions and body language, this activity requires face-to-face contact. A classroom is warranted.

The same argument applies to teaching calmness. You might be able to use Web-based simulations to simulate verbal attacks, however, thus reducing the length of classroom simulation required.

Convincing learners that disputes are destructive can be done by presenting case studies over the Web.

Objective listening requires a person, but the contact may not need to be face-to-face. Hence the Web or classroom may be appropriate.

Generally, the classroom is needed for face-to-face activities and probably will be until ultra-high-definition 3D video links are available. The Web is more than adequate for teaching any kind of verbal knowledge and for honing skills through simulated practice.

Step 3: Combining Components. Now that you have decided the possible delivery media for each component, you can decide how to combine them in a blend.

To make that decision, fall back on economic concerns. In the long run, you want to make training as inexpensive as you can and get as much revenue as possible from the expensive development efforts for e-learning components. For that reason, you want to present the items that do not require face-to-face contact in e-learning and minimize the necessary classroom time. An e-learning/

classroom/e-learning sandwich seems the best approach. Figure 9-5 shows which components will appear in each part of the sandwich.

In the first e-learning segment, learners will receive the motivation and basic skills necessary to be productive in the classroom. There they will learn that disputes are destructive and how to listen objectively. Then in the classroom segment they can apply their abilities to listen objectively as they demonstrate and hone their attitudes of openness and calmness. Finally, after returning to the workplace, they continue studying. There they learn the well-defined procedure for resolving disputes and add to their vocabulary of calming words.

Figure 9-5. Sandwich for teaching dealing with disputes among subordinates.

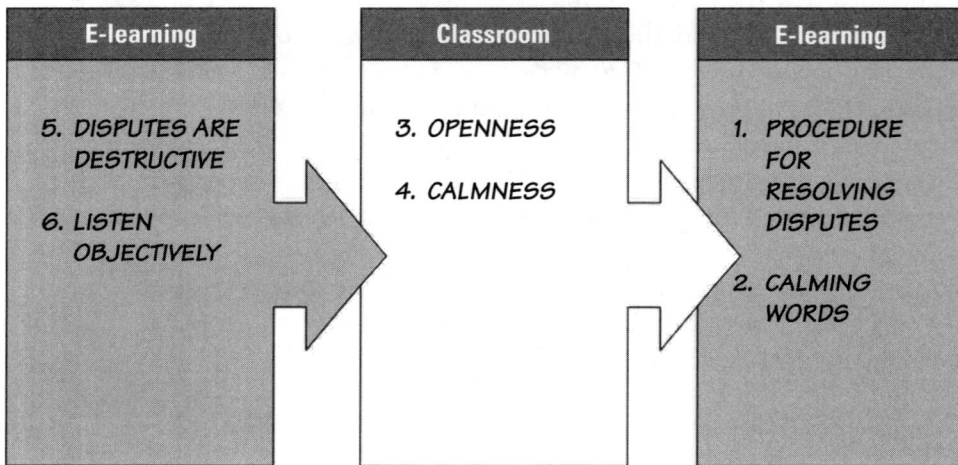

E-learning	Classroom	E-learning
5. DISPUTES ARE DESTRUCTIVE *6. LISTEN OBJECTIVELY*	*3. OPENNESS* *4. CALMNESS*	*1. PROCEDURE FOR RESOLVING DISPUTES* *2. CALMING WORDS*

◀◀ ◀◀ ◀◀ ◀◀ ◀◀ ▶▶ ▶▶ ▶▶ ▶▶ ▶▶

YOUR TURN

Now you can apply the knowledge in this chapter to plan blended solutions of your own. This activity guides you in planning one blended solution. If you have more subjects for which you want to design a blended solution, print out worksheet 9-1 or download and print out copies from this book's Website (www.horton.com/using).

Worksheet 9-1. Planning a training blend.

1. Identify a Subject for Blending

2. Explain Why Blending Is the Best Solution

3. Specify How to Teach Each Part of the Subject

Part of the subject	**How to teach it** (classroom, e-learning, or some other form)

4. Decide How to Combine Components

Describe how components are combined in the blend. Include a sketch if necessary.

10

Creating Learning Environments

Many organizations are busily stringing cable, configuring Web servers, negotiating to buy learning management systems, having consultants construct databases of knowledge resources, and connecting employees with multimedia collaboration tools. They are extending the concept of blending to include blending technologies, forms of e-learning, information products, work, and learning. When all the pieces are put together, what will the jigsaw puzzle reveal?

Without knowing it, companies are putting in place the infrastructure that makes it possible to provide every employee, manager, executive, customer, supplier, and distributor with a personal electronic learning environment.

WHAT IS A PERSONAL ELECTRONIC LEARNING ENVIRONMENT?

What exactly is a personal electronic learning environment, and what does it do for the learner? To answer these questions, start by observing how most people go about acquiring the knowledge they need to do their jobs. You will notice that one method is more common than all others.

Imagine that you need to do something new in your word processor, something you know it can do but that you have never done before and cannot figure out on your own. What do you do? If you are like 85 percent of the people in the workplace, your first choice is to ask someone: a friend, a co-worker, or a supervisor. Quite simply, most people prefer to learn by asking questions of a trusted source.

What do you want when you are stuck? Most people do not want a book or a course. They just want an answer. If they cannot ask a person, they want the computer to serve as a question-answering machine or knowledge valet. Figure 10-1 illustrates this vision.

Figure 10-1. What learners really want.

How, then, can you design systems that let people learn from their computers as a natural part of working? The answer is that you must use computers and networks to build a complete learning environment around them—an environment filled with all manner of potential learning experiences, not just e-learning courses.

WHY BUILD LEARNING ENVIRONMENTS?

Learning environments that surround learners with tools providing access to training, information, and fellow workers are expensive and difficult to construct, but they further many of the goals for e-learning presented in earlier chapters. Learning environments support and greatly simplify goals such as these:

- making learning integral to work
- increasing transfer of training to work activities
- furthering knowledge management efforts
- building learning communities within an organization
- integrating training and information efforts
- sharing infrastructure among multiple organizational efforts.

COMPONENTS OF A LEARNING ENVIRONMENT

Learning environments will be as varied as the organizations that create them. Good ones will deploy information and learning technologies to meet the unique needs of the organization. Some patterns and models, however, will be common. Look at what many learning environments will contain and how they may be configured.

Figure 10-2 shows the schematic view of a learning environment. At the center is the individual worker (a potential learner). Around the worker are the electronic mechanisms the learner can use to get the training and knowledge needed to do work, prepare for future assignments, and grow as a person. Some of these resources (those inside the circle) are within the worker's company. Others are outside. All are electronically accessible.

To keep the environment simple, the worker accesses resources through three main mechanisms: a learning management system, corporate collaboration tools, and an e-library. Here's what each one contributes:

- *Learning management system:* Access to internal classroom and e-learning courses, training portals, and external classroom courses.
- *Corporate collaboration tools:* Frequent and immediate access to peers, experts, mentors, and management though email, discussion forums, instant messaging, online meetings, and videoconferencing.
- *E-library:* Simple and direct interface to online documents, conferences, Websites, databases, and Internet searches. Also access to public newsgroups and forums frequented by peers of the worker.

Also prominent in this scheme are internal and external e-courses. These include stand-alone self-directed courses as well as courses with tools and activities to involve rich collaboration with fellow learners and a facilitator or instructor.

BUILDING AN ELECTRONIC LEARNING ENVIRONMENT

Building a learning environment requires lots of technical tasks, such as hooking together the various computers, cables, routers, and hubs, and installing and configuring software packages. But it is primarily a management chore. The technical tasks are relatively routine. Getting the required management support and budget are anything but routine.

Such a project can intimately affect how several departments do their work. Its scope can overlap the charters of several other departments. And its costs can be too high for any single department to bear. For these reasons, you will probably find that you need both top management support and gobs of interdepartmental cooperation.

Get Top Management Support

Although building a learning environment can start as a grassroots effort, it soon will need the direct support and active involvement of upper management, namely the chief executive officer. It may also require support from the chief financial officer, chief operating officer, chief knowledge officer, and the

Figure 10-2. An electronic learning environment

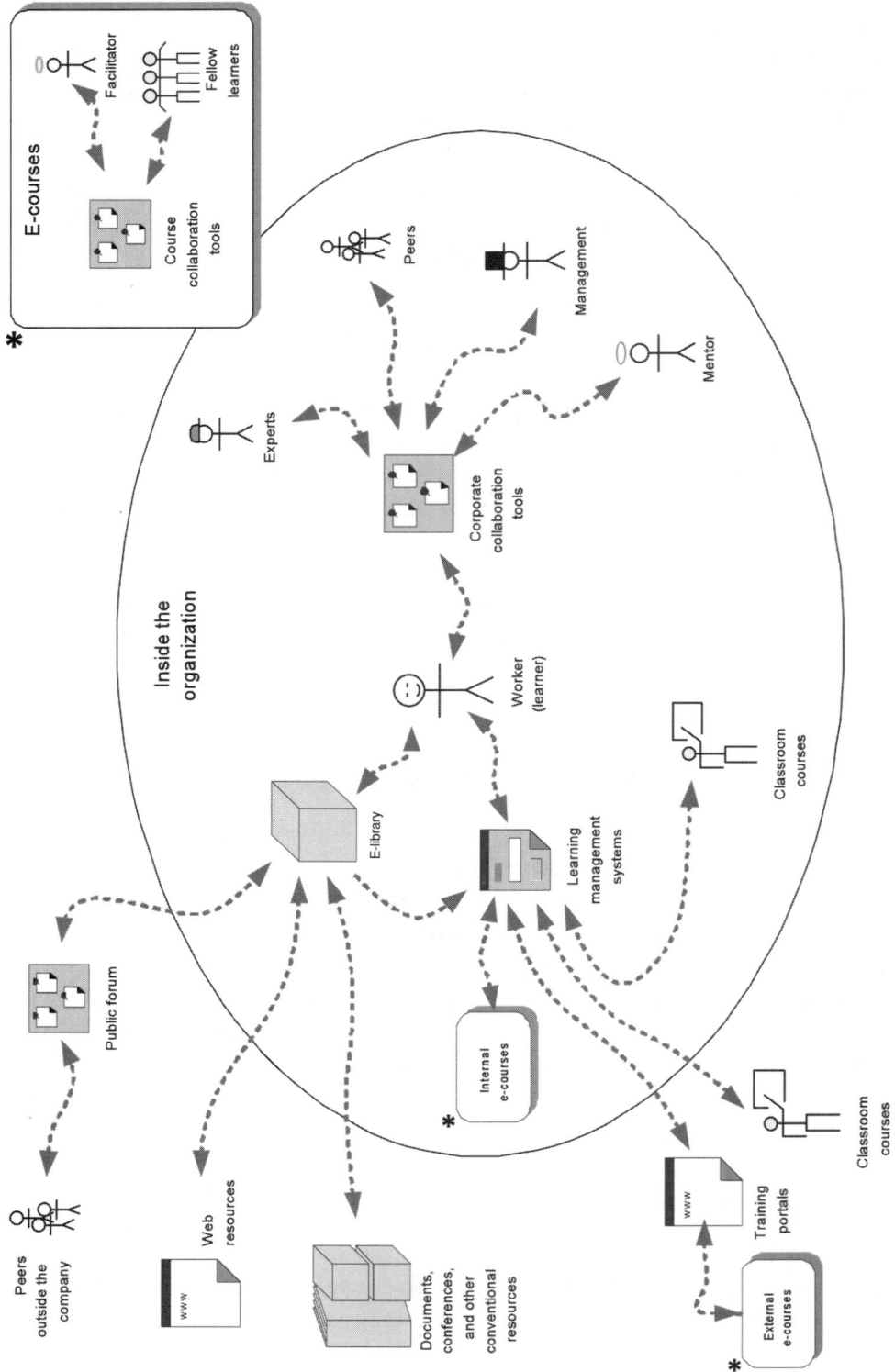

chief whatever officer. Because the learning environment will extend into all departments and even outward to customers, suppliers, distributors, regulators, and others, you will need support that spans the organization's activities.

To interest these high-level executives, point out the advantages of a learning environment for the company as a whole. Show how similar systems have streamlined operations and saved money for companies like GE, Cisco, and Oracle (Peters, 2001).

Get Everyone Working Together

Building a learning environment requires enthusiastic cooperation among departments that may not presently be aware of each other's activities and may even view the others as rivals. One of your first actions should be to contact all the potential investors and stakeholders in such a project. These include departments that benefit directly from improved learning, those that benefit from improved communications infrastructure, and those that must contribute or share resources. Potential partners in creating a learning environment include:

- e-learning (obviously)
- information technology (which owns the infrastructure)
- knowledge management projects, such as best practices, data warehousing, data mining, and so forth
- product support and internal technical support groups
- internal and external Website administrators and Webmasters
- documentation and publications departments
- organizational library department.

Make sure every participant knows What's In It For Me (WIIFM). Make every participant aware of the advantages to his or her department (better training, enhanced communications) and to him or her personally (chance to be a hero).

Clearly Demonstrate the Value of the Concept

Stress and overwork can sap the imagination of normally creative and open-minded managers. Make sure you have a way to demonstrate in simple terms what you have in mind and how it will benefit the organization.

Create a Vision Prototype. A vision prototype shows what the future could be like. A vision prototype could be a videotape demonstrating how workers will get the knowledge they need to do their jobs once a learning environment is in place. It could be an interactive demo posted on an internal Website where interested people could experience the proposed system directly. It could be a prepared slide presentation that walks people through the key elements of a learning environment in a way they can understand and appreciate.

Start in One Area to Demonstrate Value. Another way to demonstrate value is to set up a learning environment in a single area of the company. You could pick one work team, one building, or one department. Implement some of the key elements of a learning environment for workers in this area and track their improved performance as well as their reactions to the learning environment. If you do it right, you should have credible economic analyses and persuasive testimonials with which to go forward.

Show Overall Return-on-Investment

If costs and benefits are distributed over many different departments, consider calculating return-on-investment at the organizational level. Although such an analysis may be complex to perform and may take considerable time to nail down all the costs and benefits involved, it can show the cumulative effect of such a wide-ranging and expensive project.

HOW WORKERS WILL LEARN—A VISION

To create a learning environment or just to use e-learning effectively, you need more than cables and servers and software. You need a vision. It can be messy and a bit contradictory, but it needs to paint a bold picture of how e-learning can transform everyday activities of an organization. Figure 10-3 sketches a vision for what e-learning will become and how people will learn in the future.

Figure 10-3. How people will learn.

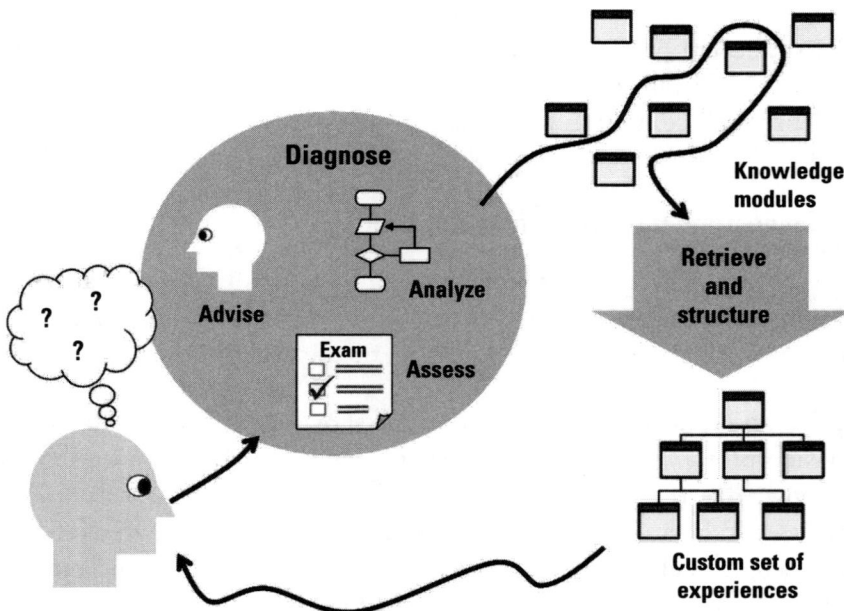

Soon each person will have access to millions or billions of knowledge modules. Some will be Webpages with simple text and graphics. Others may include multimedia simulations. Some may consist of coupons for an email exchange with a human expert, or admission to a classroom training course.

When people have a need for knowledge, they will engage a diagnostic procedure. This diagnosis may be performed in a few nanoseconds by an algorithm in their computer. Or, this diagnosis may involve taking an exam or filling out a questionnaire to assess their current knowledge level relative to their needed level. It may involve working with a counselor or adviser over a period of days.

The result of this diagnosis will be a request to a database or search engine. The needed modules will be rounded up and herded into a structure comprising a lesson or document custom tailored to the needs of the person who requested it.

This cycle of requesting and receiving knowledge may take place dozens of times a day. The custom set of experiences may take minutes or months to consume. The result, though, will be a shift from mass-manufactured to hand-crafted education.

◀◀ ◀◀ ◀◀ ◀◀ ◀◀ ▶▶ ▶▶ ▶▶ ▶▶ ▶▶

YOUR TURN

Now it is your turn to create what you think will be the learning environment of the future.

Design a Personal Learning Environment

What resources should your learners have at their disposal to obtain the training, information, and knowledge they need? In words or pictures describe your ideal electronic learning environment from the viewpoint of the individual worker.

Enunciate Your Vision

What is your vision for what e-learning should become and how people will learn in the future?

References

Ainslie, N. (1998, Spring). "Facilitated or Instructor-Led Online Learning—the Role of the Instructor." *Journal of Instruction Delivery Systems, 12*(2).

Allen, R.J. (1999). "Step Right Up! Real Results for Real People!" www.allencomm.com /software/quest/whtpgs/rexroi.html.

Anderson, J.R., Reder, L.M., and Simon, H.A. (1996). "Situated Learning and Education." *Educational Researcher, 25*(4), 5–96.

Apps, J.W. (1991). *Mastering the Teaching of Adults.* Melbourne, FL: Krieger Publishing.

ASK International. (1998). "A New Training Concept, JUST IN TIME." www.askintl .com/concept.html.

Baron, L.C., and Goldman, E.S. (1994). "Integrating Technology with Teacher Preparation." In *Technology and Education Reform,* B. Means, editor. San Francisco: Jossey-Bass.

Becker, D. (1999, 11 January). "Training On Demand." *TechWeek.* www.techweek.com.

Bernier, C.L. (1978). "Reading Overload and Cogency." *Information Processing and Management, 14,* 445–452.

Bork, A. (1997, June). "The Future of Computers and Learning." *T.H.E. Journal Online.* http://www.thejournal.com/magazine/vault/A1682.cfm.

Bransford, J.D., Brown, A.L., and Cocking, R.R., editors. (1999). *How People Learn: Brain, Mind, Experience, and School.* Washington, DC: National Academy Press.

Bransford, J.D., Franks, J.J., Vye, N.J., and Sherwood, R.D. (1989). "New Approaches to Instruction: Because Wisdom Can't Be Told." In *Similarity and Analogical Reasoning,* S. Vosniadou & A. Ortony, editors. Cambridge, UK: Cambridge University Press.

Brown, B.M. (1998, December). "Digital Classrooms: Some Myths About Developing New Educational Programs Using the Internet." *T.H.E. Journal, 26.*

Cantwell, S. (1993, November/December). "Multimedia Transforms Union Pacific's Training Strategy." *Tech Trends,* 2–3.

Carroll, J. (1990). *The Nurnberg Funnel: Designing Minimalist Instructions for Practical Computer Skill.* Cambridge, MA: MIT Press.

Chi, M.T.H., Feltovich, P.J., and Glaser, R. (1981). "Categorization and Representation of Physics Problems by Experts and Novices." *Cognitive Science, 5,* 121–152.

Crookston, J. (1999). "Meetings in America." www.teleconferencemagazine.com/november /america.htm.

deGroot, A.D. (1965). *Thought and Choice in Chess.* The Hague: Mouton.

Dempster, F. (1988, August). "The Spacing Effect: A Case Study in the Failure to Apply the Results of Psychological Research." *American Psychologist, 43,* 627–634.

Densford, L. (1998, November/December). "Sun Microsystems: Finding New Ways to Put Training in Context." *Corporate University Review,* 6.

Docent. (1999). "Lucent's Wireless University." www.docent.com/solutions/success /lucent.htm.

Drucker, P. (1994, November). "The Age of Social Transformation." *The Atlantic Monthly, 274,* 53–80.

Duchastel, P. (1997). "A Web-Based Model for University Instruction." *Journal of Educational Technology Systems, 25*(3), 221–228.

Ellis, B. (1997). "Virtual Classroom Technologies for Distance Education: The Case for On-line Synchronous Delivery." www.detac.com/solution/naweb97.htm.

Falling through the Net: Toward Digital Inclusion. (2000). Washington, DC: U.S. Department of Commerce.

Fletcher, J.D. (1990). *Effectiveness and Cost of Interactive Videodisc Instruction in Defense Training and Education.* Washington, DC: Institute for Defense Analysis.

Frand, J.L. (2000, September/October). "The Information-Age Mindset." *Educause,* 15–24.

Gery, G.J. (1991). *Electronic Performance Support Systems.* Boston: Weingarten Publications.

Gick, M.L., and Holyoak, K.J. (1983). "Schema Induction and Analogical Transfer." *Cognitive Psychology, 12,* 306–355.

Gillette, B. (1998, October). "Taking Training Online." *Corporate Meetings & Incentives.* www.meetingsnet.com.

Glaser, R. (1992). "Expert Knowledge and Processes of Thinking." In *Enhancing Thinking Skills in the Sciences and Mathematics,* D.F. Halpern, editor. Hillsdale, NJ: Erlbaum.

Glaser, R., and Chi, M.T.H. (1988). "Overview." In *The Nature of Expertise,* M.T.H. Chi, R. Glaser & M.J. Farr, editors. Hillsdale, NJ: Erlbaum.

Hall, B. (1999). *Return on Investment and Multimedia Training.* Sunnyvale, CA: brandon -hall.com.

Hall, B. (2000a, September). "E-Learning Across the Enterprise." *e-learning,* 27–34.

Hall, B. (2000b, January–March). "How to Embark on Your E-Learning Adventure." *e-learning, 1,* 10–16.

Harasim, L., Calvert, T., and Groeneboer, C. (1997). "Virtual-U: A Web-Based System to Support Collaborative Learning." In *Web Based Instruction,* B. Khan, editor. Englewood Cliffs, NJ: Educational Technology Publications.

Henry, D., Cooke, S., Buckley, P., Dumagan, J., Gill, G., and Pastore, D. (1999). *The Emerging Digital Economy II.* Washington, DC: U.S. Department of Commerce.

Hmelo, C.E. (1995). "Problem-Based Learning: Development of Knowledge and Reasoning Strategies." Seventeenth Annual Conference of the Cognitive Science Society, Pittsburgh, PA.

Horton, W. (1994). *The Icon Book: Visual Symbols for Computer Systems and Documentation.* New York: John Wiley & Sons.

Horton, W. (2001). *Leading E-Learning.* Alexandria, VA: ASTD.

Iadevaia, D. (1999, January). "An Internet-Based Introductory College Astronomy Course with Real-Time Telescopic Observing." *T.H.E. Journal, 26.*

Jonassen, D., Dyer, D., Peters, K., Robinson, T., Harvey, D., King, M., and Loughner, P. (1997). "Cognitive Flexibility Hypertexts on the Web: Engaging Learners in Meaning Making." In *Web Based Instruction,* K. Badrul, editor. Englewood Cliffs, NJ: Educational Technology Publications.

Karayan, S., and Crowe, J. (1997, April). "Student Perceptions of Electronic Discussion Groups." *T.H.E. Journal,* 69–71.

References

Klahr, D., and Carver, S.M. (1988). "Cognitive Objectives in a LOGO Debugging Curriculum: Instruction, Learning, and Transfer." *Cognitive Psychology, 20,* 362–404.

Kroder, S.L., Suess, J., and Sachs, D. (1998, May). "Lessons in Launching Web-Based Graduate Courses." *T.H.E. Journal, 25.*

Kroll, L. (1999, March 8). "Good Morning, HAL." *Forbes Magazine.* http://www.forbes.com/global/1999/0308/0205032a.html.

Larkin, J.H. (1983). "The Role of Problem Representation in Physics." In *Mental Models,* D. Gentner & A.L. Stevens, editors. Hillsdale, NJ: Erlbaum.

Lim, D.H. (1999, March). "Organizational and Cultural Factors Affecting International Transfer of Training." *Performance Improvement, 38,* 30–36.

Maher, K. (1998, August). "Inventing the Virtual Classroom." *Interactivity Magazine,* 4.

McGee, M.K. (1998, June 22). "Save On Training." *InformationWeek.* http://www.informationweek.com/688/88iutra.htm.

McGrath, B. (1998). "Partners in Learning: Twelve Ways Technology Changes the Teacher-Student Relationship." *T.H.E. Journal, 25*(9).

McNeil, J. (2001). "Americans with Disabilities 1997." http://www.census.gov/prod/2001pubs/p70-73.pdf.

Microsoft Corporation. (1998a). "San Diego State University Case Study." www.microsoft.com/education/hed/studies/caseh55.htm.

Microsoft Corporation. (1998b). "Toys 'R' Us Case Study." www.microsoft.com/Windows/NetMeeting/InAction/toysrus.asp.

Moe, M. (1999). *The Book of Knowledge: Investing in the Growing Education and Training Industry.* New York: Merrill Lynch.

Moe, M., and Blodgett, H. (2000). *The Knowledge Web.* New York: Merrill Lynch, Global Securities Research and Economics Group.

Moore, G. (1995). *Crossing the Chasm: Marketing and Selling Technology Products to Mainstream Customers.* San Francisco: Harper Business.

National Center for Policy Analysis. (2001). "Costs For Military Recruiting Skyrocket." www.ncpa.org/pi/congress/pd102299a.html.

O'Keefe, J. (1997). "Online Learning Fills Immediate Need for Employee Technology-Skills Training." www.amcity.com/albany/stories/1997/10/06/focus4.html.

Peters, T. (2001). "WebWorld2001: The 100% Solution...Now!" www.tompeters.com.

Picard, D. (1996, November). "The Future in Distance Training." *Training,* S5–S10.

Porter, P. (1999). "Boeing's Big Experiment." www.ittrain.com/archive/MarchLO_99_8.html.

Prensky, M. (1998, January). "Twitch Speed: Keeping Up With Young Workers." *Across the Board,* 14–19.

Ruch, W. (2000). "How to Keep Gen X Employees From Becoming X-Employees." www.astd.org/virtual_community/td_magazine/td_0400_contents.html.

Schaaf, D. (1998, September). "What Workers Really Think About Training." *Training Magazine,* 59–66.

Schank, R. (1995, January). "End Run to the Goal Line." *Educom Review,* 30.

Schonfeld, A.H. (1991). "On Mathematics as Sense-Making: An Informal Attack on the Unfortunate Divorce of Formal and Informal Mathematics." In *Informal Reasoning and Education,* J.F. Voss, D.N. Perkins & J.W. Segal, editors. Hillsdale, NJ: Erlbaum.

Simon, H. (1971). "Designing Organizations for an Information-Rich World." In *Computers, Communications, and the Public Interest,* M. Greenberger, editor. Baltimore: Johns Hopkins University Press.

Simon, H. (1973). "Skill in Chess." *American Scientist, 61,* 394–403.

Singley, K., and Anderson, J.R. (1989). *The Transfer of Cognitive Skill.* Cambridge, MA: Harvard University Press.

Soloway, E., Jackson, S.L., Klein, J., Quintana, C., Reed, J., Spitulnik, J., Staford, S.J., Struder, S., Eng, J., and Scala, N. (1996). "Learning Theory in Practice: Case Studies of Learner-Centered Design." CHI '96 Human Factors in Computing Systems: Common Ground, Vancouver, Canada.

Terry, L. (1998). "Slash Your Costs! Here Comes Web-Based Training." www.solutions integrator.com.

Training Magazine Staff. (1999, October). "Industry Report 1999." *Training, 36*(10), 37.

U.S. Department of Commerce. (2000). *Falling Through the Net: Toward Digital Inclusion.* Washington, DC: U.S. Department of Commerce.

Urdan, T.A., and Weggen, C.C. (2000). *Corporate E-Learning: Exploring a New Frontier.* San Francisco: WR Hambrecht + Co.

Web-Based Education Commission. (2000). *The Power of the Internet for Learning.* Washington: Web-Based Education Commission.

About the Author

William Horton has been designing technology-based training since 1971 when, as an undergraduate, he designed a network-based course for MIT's Center for Advanced Engineering Study. He also created www.DesigningWBT.com, authored e-learning courses on electronic media, and designed a network-based knowledge-management system.

A registered professional engineer and fellow of the Society for Technical Communication, William Horton is an internationally sought-after consultant and speaker and is a prolific author. His books include *Designing Web-Based Training, Designing and Writing Online Documentation,* and *Secrets of User-Seductive Documents,* as well as two more books in this series: *Leading E-Learning* and *Evaluating E-Learning.* He is co-author of *Getting Started in Online Learning* and *The Web Page Design Cookbook* and CD-ROM.